60p

Fishing
with a Purpose

By the same author

Fishing from Afar

Fishing
with a Purpose

Stephen Johnson

Foreword by Aylmer Tryon

PETER DAVIES: LONDON

Printed in Great Britain by
C. Tinling & Co. Ltd, London and Prescot

Contents

Illustrations

FOREWORD

MY OWN EDITION of the Compleat Angler includes some Commendatory Verses, and those of Christopher Harvie begin thus:—

'First mark the title well; my friend that gave it
Has made it good; this book deserved to have it
For he that views it with judicious looks,
Shall find it full of art, bait, lines and hooks.'

Fishing with a Purpose too has much to commend it for the same reasons. The author indeed lives up to the title and few, even after a late night's fishing, will lie long abed when the smell of frying finnock and bacon penetrates to their nostrils. The book strays from time to time away from the island of Skye but soon returns to his beloved Camasunary so well described in his previous book, *Fishing from Afar*, which he wrote whilst a prisoner-of-war after his Mosquito had been shot down into the sea.

All of us seek a haven to escape to from the noise and fumes of our cities, and surely the sandy bay at Camasunary, with the Cuillin Hills shielding the lochs behind the lodge, is the perfect dream of seclusion. If the weather is fine then the view of the hills and the memory-haunting light over the sea beyond Eigg and Rhum to the outer isles as the day fades is magical; if, as is usual, the rain falls, with mist on the hills, the sea-trout fishing is then wonderful—one of the many blessings of our art.

This then was the place which the father of the three Johnson brothers bought for them before the first war and which has since given immeasurable pleasure to them and their sons, and to their fortunate and grateful friends.

Whilst fishermen of all ages and skills will, I am sure, learn something from the various methods described by the author's most active and observant mind, I would

9

especially commend it to the apparently unending and unfortunate numbers who say that they are 'far too impatient to fish'. They are, if the author and his brothers will forgive me for saying so, most unlikely to be as impatient as the Johnsons. The secret is surely to catch fish of any sort by any method when beginning. I often wonder whether father Johnson had this in mind when he bought the place. When the finnock are running, which mercifully coincides with the school holidays, they will even take a fly and most certainly a worm in a spate. This impatience, too, has enriched this book with such diversity of methods, for if a salmon will not take a fly, then surely a minnow or something else will succeed. 'Try it and see' is his doctrine.

I remember watching from a bridge a fish for which Stevie Johnson was trying with a greased line. Twice the fish rose slowly to the fly. Each time in my excitement I shouted 'got him' or some similar encouraging words causing Stevie not only to strike too soon but also to emit a volley of oaths. The third time, when I had a handkerchief firmly wedged in my mouth, the fish took no notice at all.

I had hoped that the author might include a chapter on scale reading, and fear that I may be responsible for this omission. A few years ago I had caught a land-locked salmon in the Argentine. I brought back some scales and sent them to Stevie and by some strange chance they arrived on the very first day of April. 'Two years in the river and two in the sea,' was the reply. For some reason he refuses now to read the scales I send him, even on the other 364 days.

All fishing is fun and the author will, I am sure, give as much enjoyment to those who read this book as he has to those of us who have had the chance and good fortune to fish with such an enthusiast. Let us hope there will long be fish for the younger generations to catch and finnock for them to fry.

AYLMER TRYON

INTRODUCTION

There is a bewildering number of ways in which you can fish for salmon, sea-trout and brown trout. Brown trout will eat anything from a midge to a mouse and can be caught on the natural beastie or on artificial imitations. Salmon can be tempted by imitations of everything edible they met in the sea or in rivers before they went to the sea. This gives tackle makers great opportunities. Salmon seldom take anything but there are hundreds of things they might take. Fishing tackle shops are full of them, with plenty more to come. The man who only fishes with a fly can walk past the cases full of minnows, spoons, prawns, sprats and plugs; but he still has an alarming selection of flies to choose from, and an ever-increasing variety of methods and depths at which he can fish them.

For the last twenty years I have lived in the Tweed Valley and been lucky enough to fish many different beats. I have also fished for salmon on the Spey, Tay, Dee, Eden, and in Ireland and Iceland. I have tried to fish by whatever method was the most likely to catch something. I have also talked to people who are experts in different methods, and tried to absorb their knowledge and emulate their skill.

This I find quite fascinating and it has added greatly to my pleasure in going fishing. Perhaps I can record some of the things I have learnt and some of the fun I have had.

January, 1969   S.P.L.J.

I

ABOUT FISHERMEN

YOU CAN TAKE up fishing at any age, but the mad keen
fisherman is born that way. He cannot cross any bridge
without looking at the river which flows beneath it.

However often you fish during a season, and for however
many years, the urge remains. Sometimes you may think
that you have worked it out of your system; but this is
purely temporary. At the end of the season on the Tweed,
in the short dark days of December you may just be able to
say, 'Well really I am quite glad that it's over.' But some
people can't even do that, and they gaze at the river with
longing even in the closed season.

You may put your rod away, almost with relief, but after
two months of forced rest you will be as keen as a schoolboy back for his holidays. Your perseverance may be
affected, as you will feel the cold of February more when
you get older. You may not actually run the last hundred
yards to the first pool you are going to fish, but you will
quite definitely hurry. I never put my rod up until I am
in sight of the river so that I can watch and listen for a
fish jumping while getting everything ready.

So a new season starts with all the tremendous variety
that fishing can offer. Each aspect has its own fascination
and appeal. Salmon fishing in the spring when trees are
bare and there is snow on the hills: trout rising all over a
run when there is a hatch of dark olives on a rough northern stream in April: May and June when the calm evening
waters of a hill loch or chalk stream are alive with the rings

of rising trout: July, August and September are the months of the sea-trout with these wonderful fish running up every burn and river in the Western Highlands and islands; the soft rain lashing down from low scudding clouds and the hills loud with the roar of many waters. The variety is such that no one could ever tire of fishing, but there is also a basic purpose to it. Fishing is no pointless sport, for our game fish are the finest eating there is. You look forward to your first salmon steak, your first smoked trout, your first sea-trout finnock with bacon for breakfast with the same anticipation each year.

No wonder fishermen are so keen, for the thrill of catching and the pleasure of eating are closely linked. It is our very keenness which sometimes brings out the less attractive sides of our characters, and this we should be aware of and guard against. Above all, if you are a fisherman you must also be a sportsman, and a sportsman is one who does not interfere with another man's sport. What is more he must respect other people's feelings and abide by the will of the majority and any rules they make even if he thinks they are illogical.

On some salmon rivers there is a rule that you may only fish with a fly. Many people think that there is no pleasure in catching a salmon by any other method, and that bait fishing may put salmon off taking a fly. This may be so under low water conditions, particularly on a small river, but this attitude can also be the selfish one of men who are experts with a fly rod, cannot fish well with a bait and refuse to learn to do so.

More fish will be caught if there is no restriction on angling methods, but let us always remember that salmon start with one great advantage over the angler. They do not feed in fresh water and cannot digest anything they swallow. For this reason the number of salmon caught by fair rod fishing, using any fly or lure you like, will never seriously deplete the number of salmon left to spawn in any river system.

I fish with a bait when it is permitted, because I become disheartened by fishing with a fly if absolutely nothing happens for several hours. However lovely the view, my primary object in going fishing is to catch something. The sun shines more brightly and the birds sing more sweetly for me when I have a salmon on the bank.

If you decide to use a bait an absorbingly interesting problem is immediately presented. There are so many different lures and baits on which salmon have been caught and many ways of presenting each and every one of them. You only have one pair of hands and the day is short. What are you going to try and how long are you going to persevere with each before changing to something different, always remembering the time it takes to make a change?

If by your efforts you manage to catch a salmon, when you would not have done so with a fly, you will have achieved something, and you may have learnt something about the taking habits of these most unpredictable fish. The more skilful you are at all the methods you employ the greater is your chance of success.

A mistake which some people make is to formulate a theory of why and when fish take and then try and fit the salmon's behaviour into their own rules. In order to learn you must keep an open mind. Observe all you can, ask questions and pick the brains of experts, who are usually only too willing to tell you how they catch salmon. Never become dogmatic or be influenced by people who are, or by the books they write. The fascination lies in continuing to increase your knowledge of what fly or lure a salmon is most likely to take, at different times of the year, in different rivers and under varying conditions. A pattern will eventually emerge, but be sure this will keep altering for as long as you keep an open mind. In the words of a Spey gillie: 'You never know, and when you think you know you are never sure.'

One of the most difficult tasks a keen angler has to face

is that of maintaining a Christian attitude to his rival anglers on all occasions. It is a pity that rivers must have two banks and that they form such convenient boundaries between properties. It just isn't true that all fishermen are charming fellows, any more than it is true that everyone who drives a car is quite delightful. Indeed it is a sad fact that a steering wheel and a rod in some people's hands can have much the same adverse effect. Fishing should bring out the best in all of us but the sight of a strange angler on the opposite bank, especially if he is carrying a fish while we have none, is apt to do the opposite. 'The enemy' or 'the opposition' are two of the more polite methods of alluding to the fellow on the other side.

When you have caught a number of fish in your lifetime it should surely become possible for even the keenest angler to take pleasure in watching someone else catch a fish, especially if he is a novice. This is easy enough if he is one of your family or a friend, and should still not be impossible if he is a stranger.

Once before the dam was built I was fishing the top pool on the River Awe. I had to cross over the bottom of Loch Awe in the Pass of Brander by boat to fish the left bank. After a while another angler appeared on the other bank. I waved to him and he waved back. I observed that he was fishing with a 10 ft. trout rod and wondered what would happen if he hooked a River Awe monster.

We fished away, and after half an hour he hooked a fish and appeared very excited about it.

'Do you want any help in gaffing it?' I shouted across to him.

'Well that is awfully kind of you,' he replied. 'Actually I haven't got a gaff.'

I welcomed the break in my fruitless efforts, put down my rod, and rowed across to his side with my gaff. He was on a steep bank above deep water. He told me that it was the first salmon he had ever hooked. His enthusiasm and excitement were infectious. Fortunately the fish wasn't more than about 10lb. and he was playing it very nicely. There were some bushes on the bank and we had our anxious moments. His rod was so short that he had difficulty in getting the line over the top of the bushes when the salmon ran up or down past a clump. Once he leaned out so far that I thought he must fall in, but all went well, and with only a few unnecessary words of advice he brought the fish in to the side and I gaffed it. Well, he was absolutely thrilled. He couldn't take his eyes off it as he laid it lovingly in the back of his car. He thanked me profusely and offered me a bit of it. Then he said he thought he had had enough excitement for one day, took his rod down and drove away.

I rowed back and began fishing again, quite without success, but I had had the fun of sharing in his excitement. A quarter of an hour later a large car drew up opposite me and an elderly man with a red face got out.

'Has anybody been fishing here?' he shouted across to me.

'Yes, there was someone,' I said.

'Well, he had no right to be; he was poaching,' he said very crossly. 'This fishing belongs to the hotel and I have taken it for the day. He didn't catch one, did he?'

'Yes, he did as a matter of fact, a beauty,' I said.

His face became like the sun setting on a foggy night. I thought I had better not tell him of my part in the affair or he might burst. I suppose my successful friend had heard some loose talk in the tartan upholstered hotel bar the previous night, when the red-faced gentleman had announced grandly that he had taken the salmon fishing but would be a bit late starting next morning.

I must admit that I take a lenient view of those who occasionally poach for the sport or the pot; but not of those who do so to make money. There is no thrill quite like catching a salmon and eluding the owner and river watchers; but you must be young and active. You should however always ask permission to fish first. If you are in a remote part of the Highlands and you are refused, then you can poach, if not with a clear conscience, at least with some justification.

We all think that we want to fish the best beats on the best rivers and catch a great number of salmon; but then we all think that we want to be very rich. In neither case does it necessarily lead to happiness. There is a greater thrill in catching one salmon where they are scarce and seldom caught than in catching any one fish from a prolific beat.

Recently in an hotel in Kelso I heard a man asked how he had got on fishing that day. 'Poor,' he said, 'I only got four.' Then on my way home I passed a man I knew riding a bicycle, a salmon's tail sticking out of the game-bag on his back. He grinned broadly when I waved to him.

The fewer fish you catch the keener you become to get one. You begin to cook it the moment you hook it. This is a mistake for it nearly always gets off. If on the other hand you eventually manage to take one of those super beats we all long to fish, it is so expensive that you can ill afford the rent. You can think of little but the cheque you hope to get from the fishmonger as you add another fish to the heap in the bottom of the boat. If you don't catch any fish the gloom is awful. What is more you must fish from 10 a.m. to 5 p.m. whatever the weather is like, even if there is an easterly wind howling up the river with frequent snow showers and you are completely numb.

If you fish a poor and inexpensive beat you can at least afford to go home and get into a hot bath when things become unbearable. The man in the hotel had worked out that he had to catch and sell six fish a day to pay his rent, so four was a bad day, poor chap. He probably couldn't afford to eat one, or only ate the baggits (inedible unspawned females) like one man I know.

My friend on the bicycle had only paid two pounds for his season's fishing on the Association water. One rule is that you may not sell your fish, so he was hurrying home

in time for his wife to cook it for his tea. On this day anyway there would be no word of his wasting his time by
going fishing, and I am sure she would cook it very well too.

As you get older you have to watch yourself; my goodness you do. It is so easy to become selfish and disillusioned
and derive no pleasure from what should be the most
pleasant of sports. You can unfortunately see examples of
what you may become all too frequently. I know one
elderly man who fishes a great deal and has never given
away a day's fishing in his life. He looks and is miserable.
If you are getting older you can so easily recapture the
excitement and enthusiasm of youth by inviting young
people to fish, and sharing their thrills and triumphs.

You meet all kinds of behaviour on the banks of a river,
but the worrying thing is that the people concerned never
think they are behaving oddly. They always put the blame
on the other fellow.

In Scotland the salmon fishing rights and trouting rights
on the same stretch often belong to different people. Just
after the war a friend of mine obtained permission to fish
for trout on the Tweed just below Cornhill. He had been
wounded and a prisoner-of-war for a short while. There
was still rationing and we were all a bit hungry. He began
fishing down a run behind but nearly opposite a boat
containing a boatman, who was rowing, and a lady who
was wielding a salmon rod. There were a lot of salmon
showing, and quite soon my friend Bob hooked one on his
trout fly. When he saw what had happened the boatman
became extremely interested and rowed across to catch
him poaching red-handed.

'What are you up to?' he asked aggressively when he
came up.

'I have permission to fish for trout,' replied Bob. 'If a
salmon takes my fly I can't help it. You can net it if you
like.'

'Well, we'll see,' said the boatman. He duly netted the
fish and was swift to look in its mouth. He found a trout-

sized March Brown, perhaps on the large size but undoubtedly tied for trout.

'You had better put it back,' said Bob.

'Not bloody likely,' said the boatman, whacking it on
the head with a priest. 'We'll just keep this and see what
Mr Bloggs has to say when he comes down.'

They got themselves sorted out and all began fishing
again. Quite soon Bob hooked another salmon. He landed
three altogether while the lady in the boat caught none.

'I don't know what Mr Bloggs will say,' was the boatman's comment as he dispatched the third and put it in
the boat.

Mr Bloggs eventually arrived and they all forgathered to
hear what the great man's verdict would be. He was a
large, well-fed gentleman smoking a cigar. He listened in
silence while the boatman told him what had happened
and asked what should be done with the fish.

Mr Bloggs answered without hesitation, 'Put 'em in
back o' Bentley,' and turning to Bob he said, 'Well done,
lad, you've had the fun of catching 'em.'

A few years later a somewhat similar thing happened to
Bob but rather the other way round. He was fishing for
trout on the Teviot in the summer, and as he walked under
a bridge he found a small boy of about eight sitting by one
of the arches crying his eyes out.

'What's the matter?' he asked.

'I've hooked a fish,' said the little boy.

'Well what's so terrible about that?' asked Bob.

'I don't think I ought. I haven't permission to fish,' said
the boy with a sob.

'That's perfectly all right,' said Bob. 'Any child under
fourteen is allowed to fish for trout without paying.' This
is indeed the excellent rule of our local association.
'Where's your rod?'

The boy stopped howling and began sniffing. 'Here,' he
said, picking up a pitch-black greenheart, about 7 ft. long,
with a small brass reel, and on it some of that undressed,

multi-coloured line, which he had tried to hide under some grass in his misery.

Bob took the rod and reeled in. He expected to come in contact with a small trout or an eel, but when the line came tight he found that the boy had hooked a salmon.

'Here, take it,' he said, holding the rod out to the boy.

'No, Mister. I don't know how. Please you do it,' said the boy.

Bob tightened just sufficiently to make the salmon take a little exercise. He didn't know what tackle the boy was fishing with, but suspected the worst. He soon found out that there was only about twenty yards of line on the reel when the salmon made a run and the note it emitted became a high pitched oil-less shriek. Bob had to move quickly and run as fast as he could until the fish stopped. He then asked the boy about the tackle between himself and the fish. The nylon and hooks belonged to the boy's Dad. They had been unearthed from the back of a drawer before they set off with Mum on a camping holiday on Dad's motor-bike and side-car. Dad himself hadn't fished for some twenty years. What the knots were like that held things together Bob didn't dare consider. There was no need to enquire about the bait. Bob had noticed its pals wriggling about in a rusty tin.

Fortunately it wasn't *that* large a fish and it was more or less confined to the deep hole behind the pillar of the bridge, where it had been lying. With a deal of luck and considerable skill Bob at last managed to beach it and get it ashore. It was rather thin and rather red, but not to one pair of eyes.

'Ooh,' said the boy, gazing at the gleaming monster.

'Here, take it, it is yours,' said Bob.

The boy's eyes got bigger and bigger. 'Can I really?' he asked.

When last seen he was hurrying off across a field towards a rather small off-white tent. He was half-carrying, half-dragging the fish. Sometimes he tried to run and sometimes he had to pause and rest.

2

ABOUT FISH

FROM AN ANGLING point of view no time spent in watching fish is wasted. All your observations will eventually build up into a knowledge of fish behaviour which will help you to predict fishes' reactions and increase the chances of your catching them. Lesson One you can learn from the humble gold fish in its suburban bowl. At feeding time pop in a small piece of silver paper instead of the expected ant's egg and observe what happens. See just how long the little fish keeps it in its mouth before it notices that silver paper doesn't taste right and blows it out again. This gives a very fair indication of the time it takes for a brown trout to do exactly the same thing with an artificial fly.

Spend as much time as you can leaning over bridges watching trout or salmon in the water below.

When you have watched salmon and trout for a number of years you will be able to form an opinion, if you see a fish, whether it is likely to take a fly or not. Here are two examples: A trout which you see rising regularly to natural flies will probably take your artificial fly if an acceptable pattern is well presented to him: a salmon in a highland pool at mid-day in low water, which is lying completely motionless beside a boulder, will show no interest in anything—he is indeed so oblivious to his surroundings that he is surprisingly easy to poach.

The motions of the fish will tell you whether it is likely to take or not. A fish without movement will never do so. In still water trout and sea-trout must be on the move to be on the feed. In moving water they must be active-looking and preferably high in the water. Shoals of sea-trout in the sea waiting for a spate to run up a river, move about the bay fairly rapidly when they are on the take. Sometimes at dead low tide a shoal may become quite motionless in shallow water. You can see their dorsal fins cutting the surface, and being drifted about by the tide like pieces of sea-weed. Then they will pay not the smallest attention to a fly; only if alarmed will they move away. The same applies to trout in lochs. If you see a motionless fish you needn't bother to fish for it, but you don't often see fish in lochs and have to judge their movements by their rises. Loch Coruisk in Skye is one place where you can, under certain conditions of light, see fish from a boat, swimming slowly about without being alarmed. You can see them come up from 5 or 6ft. and take a fly. They look surprisingly brown in the water, and white when they come to your fly as you then see their tummies.

To see and watch trout in less clear water you need a loch with a steep bank and overhanging trees. There was just such a loch in Selkirkshire where you could watch for a cruising trout and then fish for it. The water was rather green and cloudy with algae so you couldn't see the trout for long. If the trout were on the feed, and you watched for a while, a fish of anything up to three pounds would swim slowly past beneath the overhanging beech trees. Sometimes you saw him rise, but even if you didn't you knew for certain that he was on the take. You had to keep perfectly still while he was in sight; but once he had gone, you climbed swiftly over the fence and got ready with a fly suspended a few inches above the surface. There you sat until he reappeared, and this might be from any direction. You could only move your eyes without frightening him; but if you kept perfectly still you appeared to him like a tree stump. Your rod was a branch and the fly, if it landed a foot or so from him, was something edible that had conveniently fallen out of the tree. The pattern of dry fly didn't matter much; it looked so realistic suddenly appearing like that with no nylon touching the water that it was almost irresistible. The trout would always turn and swim slowly towards it as he inspected it. Right at your feet he looked enormous; then he usually deliberately opened his mouth and took it. On a really short line you have to wait quite a time after the fly disappears before striking. If you judged it correctly, action was immediate. There was one tremendous splash from the fish, a flurry of flying water, and then the reel screamed as the fish made for the underwater snags of dead branches where he often broke the cast. Calm descended once more on the scene, and when your heart had stopped beating so wildly you went and looked for another cruising fish.

In running water fish must also have an active look about them to be on the take. They must be balanced delicately in the current with their pectoral fins just moving. If you watch closely you can tell instantly when a bad cast alarms them. They go still for a moment and sink an inch or two in the water and then they continue moving but with a slightly different motion. One more bad cast and they are off, so it is better to let them settle for quite a while before casting again.

This applies to salmon as well as trout. A salmon lying fairly high in the water with an active balanced look about him should excite you at once. There is a very good chance that if you present him with an acceptable lure he will take it. I don't think that the salmon which swim around a large pool on a summer's evening will take; but before they begin on their swim round the pool or start running up to the next pool they become active for a short while, and it is then that they are most likely to take. Salmon take far less frequently than trout and you can seldom see the fish for which you are fishing without him seeing you, although it is often possible to see the fish someone else is fishing for. It is most exciting doing this, and you can learn a lot from observing the look of salmon which do and do not take. After a while you can predict when a salmon is likely to do so. He must react to the fly or lure which is being presented to him; a gradual increase in activity is a good sign. Once he becomes active he will eventually take or become frightened and leave his lie if you keep on at him. If he pays not the smallest attention go and look for another fish. A prawn is the lure which salmon are least likely to ignore; but it is more likely to frighten a fish than catch him. A worm is probably the best bait for teasing a fish into taking—keep it about six inches in front of his nose for a few minutes and even the most motionless fish will begin to stir. His pectoral fins will begin to twitch, he may swim away and come back, and then without warning he will open that great mouth and suck in the worm. You generally need an accomplice observing and directing operations, and it is much more fun if there are two of you. When he sees the worm disappear he will yell 'Strike!' and when you do you will almost certainly fail to hook the fish!

When you watch fish there is always a desire to have them in your hands. A hill burn is the best place to satisfy this wish. The first fish that humans ever caught must have been with their bare hands and there is still a great satisfaction in doing so. If you walk quietly up the bank of a small burn you will see surprisingly big trout scurrying up and down. They eventually go to ground under stones or overhanging bits of the bank, often leaving a muddy disturbance in the water at the point where they have disappeared. I am no expert at tickling trout but you want to explore a hole very, very slowly and gently with the tips of the fingers. The first two or three fish will shoot off when you touch them, but keep on trying until you find one that doesn't. Then try and get your fingers just behind his gills and pin him to the stone or bank and squeeze hard. It is great sport for children on a warm summer's day. I was watching my boys doing it last year when an enormous eel shot out of a hole that Bill had his hand in.

The most exciting place to watch salmon and sea-trout is where they are jumping up a waterfall. You can often get quite close to them and for a moment they may be within reach ... Watching the caulds on Border streams there is usually a small group of men and boys; hidden nearby is an assortment of hooks and gaffs. Watching the group of men and boys are the Tweed baillies. At waterfalls on Highland rivers, during a run of fish, sea-gulls often wait for the occasional fish which falls back and stuns itself.

If you watch for long enough you can also learn a lot about how fish run. After any great effort they must rest for a while; the greater the effort the longer they rest. This they can do on a surprisingly steep sloping smooth rock with a really quick glide of water over it. I have lain on a rock and put my hand gently down among sea-trout resting in just such a place. When you touch them they move quietly away and it is impossible to grip one.

Catching fish in your bare hands is quite the most difficult thing to do if the fish has plenty of water to swim around in. It is also the most thrilling way of getting a fish that I know. I have only once caught a salmon in this way and it is most unlikely that I shall ever do so again. The experience is like that right and left at woodcock.

It was in Skye that it happened and there was a spate in the Camasunary river. The boys had been fishing the falls pools in the morning and were off on some other ploy, so Brenda and I were allowed the tin of worms. The river had fallen in a little, but there was still a roar of white water and spray among the boulders at the foot of the main fall. Here the sea-trout rest a while and will often take a worm in the quiet water behind rocks. Brenda was fishing away when I saw a salmon jump up the main fall with a tremendous effort and make its way up the steep gliding

water into a little ease quite near the bank. I scrambled
and waded across to a little island as quickly as I could, for
that fish would only rest for a short time. I stalked up the
wet rock behind it on all fours and could see its tail showing
from time to time in the white water, but it saw me and
made a rush up the steep water ahead of it. I thought it
was the end of my hopes yet the fish hadn't quite got the
energy to make it and it dropped back to its original
position. Keeping much lower this time and kneeling in the
running water with my gum-boots quite full I reached out
my hand, gripped the fish just above the tail and snatched
at the same time. Brenda who didn't know that I had left
her side was startled by the sight of a salmon sailing
through the air—but not as startled as the salmon which
had left its violent reactions until too late, and was flapping
madly on the rocks behind me. I slithered down and pinned
him before he could escape, and it was salmon for supper.

3

FLY-FISHING FOR TROUT

WHEN I GO fishing for trout I like to enjoy myself and to catch enough fish for the household needs, with perhaps a few to give away. I can usually achieve this in the most pleasant way I know of fishing for trout, with a fly. For this reason I seldom fish by any other method.

The River Jed runs past our garden and several miles of it are part of our Association water. When the boys are home for the holidays they demand trout for breakfast about three times a week, for the Jed trout are exceptionally good eating. I keep a rod up in the porch and usually contrive an hour's fishing at the time of day when I think the trout will rise best.

Catching trout on the Jed when the water is low is a fairly advanced form of angling. It requires all one's knowledge, concentration and skill. For the first few years I was up here I failed dismally and told my wife that it was impossible. The problem is not in finding a rising trout, but in finding one which you can approach without scaring a dozen others you haven't seen. These rush off up-stream and frighten the fish you were approaching so carefully. Casting isn't easy either as there are trees everywhere and the river often runs through a tunnel of branches.

This is perhaps why so few of the young now fish with a fly. The first tackle they buy is a fibreglass rod, a fixed spool reel and a Mepps spinner. They walk quickly from pool to pool having a few chucks into each. This is such a pity because men of the older generation of Borderers

are still some of the finest trout fishers you will find
anywhere. Nor do the young enjoy fishing with their
spinning rods nearly as much as they would if they used
fly rods. They become bored after half an hour or so and
go home. They prick a lot and catch only a few, although,
contrary to popular belief, they do not denude the river
of fish; there are still far too many small fish in the water.
This overstocking is due to the river having good spawning
beds, while the Hawick Association, which has the water
above the Jed Forest Association, puts in a lot of small
trout. They have a hatchery and have to justify it by
putting their wretched little fish somewhere.

I always talk to the boys I meet and try to persuade
them to take up fly-fishing. By way of encouragement
I show them what I have caught, as I usually have more
than they, and I show them my flies and offer to teach
them how to make them. They are polite but not in the
least interested.

But what they miss! The young anglers on the Jed are
remarkably accurate with their casting and land their
Mepps spoons within inches of branches and rocks with
complete confidence. They touch a number of fish that
they don't see and hook one occasionally. With spinning
you really do chuck and chance it.

Fly-fishing is so very different. It is a challenge, for it
takes a lifetime to become in any way proficient. With wet
or dry fly you nearly always see the fish take even if the
water is a bit coloured after a spate. You will see the trout
appear in the golden brown water and with a little flick
take your fly, then you will feel that thrilling tug, tug . . .
When the river is low you see your tiny dry fly bobbing
down a fast rocky run and disappear when the trout you
can also see rises and takes it. This and the skill needed to
put the fly in the right place are the thrills of fly-fishing
for trout.

Trout can be very difficult or quite easy to catch on a
fly. I like to start beginners when the river has just run in

after a flood in April. There is usually a good rise of hungry and not-too-critical trout to dark olive nymphs from mid-day until tea-time. If there is a little colour in the water they are not too fussy about the pattern of fly or the occasional splash from a bad cast. I choose a run where there are no trees to complicate matters and get the boy to cast out and across the stream as lightly as he can. The current straightens the line, and if he holds the rod still the fly fishes round through the stream quite attractively. Almost certainly a complete novice will have several rises, and with any luck a trout will hook itself. Fishing in this way you miss a high percentage of the trout you rise, but this doesn't matter to the beginner; at least he has the thrill of a pull.

For a lifetime of enjoyment the young should be taught to cast a fly and tie one at an early age.

When learning to cast you need the advice and tuition of an expert. The amateur fisherman is seldom as good a caster as he thinks he is. If you go to a professional, who competes in competitions, he will probably teach you to cast better, more quickly than a helpful amateur; but he may not know as much about catching fish.

I don't think you can go past fibreglass rods for beginners, and many very experienced fishermen use them. But make sure that the one you buy hasn't got too stiff a top joint, a common fault with many, and it makes casting very difficult. One advantage of these rods is that they are practically unbreakable, another is that they are cheap, which appeals to most of us these days.

When you first learn to tie a fly you imitate the ones that other people make, but you will soon want to make patterns that are all your own. Later on you will tie your flies exactly the way you want them, and most will be quite unlike any you find in shops. In this part of the world you simply cannot buy imitations of the very small flies which you see fish taking in the summer on our lochs and streams. For any one part of the country, you need far fewer patterns than the display cabinets in shops would indicate, and a full and varied fly-tin is unfortunately no passport to success. Nor do you need very much equipment for tying your flies. In early spring, March and April, by far the commonest fly on the water is a medium-sized dark olive. I don't know its Latin name, nor the names of any other flies, but I know exactly what they look like and how to tie an imitation which the trout will take. A Greenwell's Glory and a Water-hen are the best replicas of this particular fly, the Water-hen resembling the nymph. Tie it with primrose silk, which should not be too clean for the olive body; a little mole hair dubbing and a feather from the inside of a water-hen's wing for the hackle. Incidentally the water-hen also makes very good soup. A Greenwell you can buy in any shop, and copy. The hackle is called 'Furnace'. You can get a neck of these from Venniard, who will supply anything you cannot collect yourself. All my wings I make from starling wing feathers and there are flocks of starlings in plenty.

As in learning anything, the way to start is with a demonstration, then practice and further demonstration. It is difficult to learn from reading; but I have picked up a few tips which I find useful. At some time or other teach yourself to tie flies not only with a table vice, but also with a hand vice and with no vice at all. Except when tying small trout flies never use the silk which tackle shops sell for the job. Instead use rod-whipping silk which is much stronger, and will not break at a critical moment. Thread the silk through the centre of the reel, undo as much as you will need for one fly and slip it into the nick in the wood. You can then let go of the silk, and the weight of the reel stops the silk from coming undone. Never use those awful hackle pliers, but get a small pair of human artery forceps which close absolutely accurately, and don't slip off the hackle. When making a wing, a pair of dissecting forceps are very useful for picking up the two pieces of wing that you have cut from the starling wing, placing them side by side, and picking them both up together. Don't be surprised or unduly worried if your wings don't go on straight. They may eventually after much practice, but in the meantime you will be more worried by the crooked wings than the fish will. There is, however, a method of putting them on straight. Before putting the silk over the wing, loop it round the little finger of your hand which is holding the wing in position. Then put the silk over the wing with a loose loop above it and down the far side. Holding the wing tight in position with thumb and forefinger, pull the silk down from the near side with your little finger until it is tight. Next pull down from the far side until the silk is tight, then remove you little finger and pull the last loop tight. This is so much easier to demonstrate than describe. Finally use ladies' colourless nail varnish when you want to make things secure, and at all times plenty of sticky colourless wax on your tying silk.

When describing sizes of flies anywhere in this book I have omitted numbers from a scale. This is because each hook manufacturer uses a different scale and so numbers are completely misleading. I have published letters and articles and spoken in public, imploring manufacturers to get together and standardise a scale, but with no success. Trout sizes are not quite so chaotic as salmon sizes, but it is surely a pretty silly situation when a No. 6 may be a No. 4 or No. 8 on someone else's scale. If they would only give us the lengths in millimetres corresponding to their numbers we should know where we were. But meanwhile I for one have stopped trying to alter things.

You can catch fish on a fly when there is a lot of colour and sometimes when the river is rising rapidly. The secret then is to fish right in close to the bank in the eddies behind tufts of grass. Even for experienced anglers it is great fun sometimes to fish for fish that are fairly easy to catch just after a flood. Under ideal conditions on the Jed or Tweed in April you can catch about forty trout in a day without much difficulty. The numbers you catch and the ease of catching them decreases when the water clears and falls in.

In coloured water I fish with two flies, usually a Green-well's and a Water-hen, one size larger than I use in clear water. I fish them across the stream or up and across, and let them float down the stream naturally. To do this I follow the line down with the rod top. When they begin to drag I either cast again or, if the current isn't too swift, let the flies swim through the current to below me. You don't feel a fish take if the fly isn't dragging, so you have to watch for your line to stop or for a rise or flash in the water. Strike at once if you have any indication that a fish may have risen to your fly. If you hesitate for a second you will be too late to hook him.

In a big water on a small river you can fish the long pools which are normally too still. The flow will be sufficient to bring your flies round with enough but not too much motion through the water. I wear thigh boots and wade carefully and slowly down-stream, close in to the bank. It is important not to make ripples. If you are beneath overhanging trees you have to switch cast, but remember to strike sideways, too, or when you miss the fish your fly will be wrapped round a branch out of reach. Even if you have alarmed trout when getting into position to fish a pool, they will recover quickly if a number of flies begin coming down, so stand still for a few moments and see what happens. Trout may suddenly start rising all over the place in spite of your presence, and you can often catch several without moving. If you can find some slack water beyond the current and cast into it, holding your line high so it doesn't drag too much, you can often take several fish from the one spot. The current seems to hide you from them.

When you see fish rising to surface flies you may do better to change over to fishing with a dry fly; but at first it is a good idea to keep on one wet fly and put on one dry fly so that you can see which the fish prefer. They frequently take both equally readily. It is also an advantage always to grease your line. A greased line is better than an Air Cel line because it is visible on the surface and you can see the second it stops when a fish takes.

When the river runs in small in May and June, trout become very difficult to catch, but I love the hot still afternoons spent by the little river; the sun and the shadows, the green trees and countryside, the blue sky and distant hills, the sparkling waters over bright many-coloured stones.

If you aren't too proud to fish for wild little trout from 8 ins. to 10 ins. long on our Border streams, you will find them just as difficult as chalk stream trout to catch.

The secret of success is to know and recognise the places where it is possible to rise a trout on a dry fly. You will never catch one in the middle of a large still pool. They are indeed full of fish as you can see. But however carefully you approach, and however accurately you cast you are bound to frighten some which will scare the rest. You will see fish rising, but even if you get within casting distance of one and land your fly delicately within inches of his nose, he will have far too long to criticise and spurn your imitation of the flies he has been swallowing so happily. You can fish such places all day and never even nearly rise a trout. The only fish you may rise in such a place are at the bottom and very top of the pool.

If you approach a pool by wading over the shallows from below, you may be able to spot the fish nearest to you, and you will have disturbed no others to cover him. Kneel in the shallow water and cast your fly into the quickening glide where he is lying. Unfortunately your line will land in the more rapidly flowing broken water, and the fly will drag almost at once, but there is just a chance, if you throw a controlled crooked cast, of rising that trout.

The run at the top of the pool is a much more likely place to rise a trout. There will be fish right up in the thin rapid water, and they will have less time to scrutinise your fly. If there is a good natural hatch of flies, an artificial one bobbing down such a place can be almost irresistible. Any fish which you disturb when getting into position should come back down past you, making for the main pool, and will not worry the ones further up. You often find the best fish in these places and the biggest one of all may be at the very top, so fish up into the breaking water.

The most rewarding places are the long quick shallows among rocks and boulders. If you stalk up them quietly you will discover little easy places where the water is a few inches deeper, unbroken but still swift flowing. These will all hold two or three good trout which are approachable and possible to catch. Fish them carefully even if you can't see the trout. A gravel-bed on the edge or in midstream sometimes helps. Kneel well back from it and cast the fly just beyond, letting the line land on the gravel. There will probably be a fish right in at the edge, and these fish often take.

The flies that hatch at this time of year, and which the fish take, are very small and look creamy white. I tie mine on an appropriate-sized hook so that they look the right size when on the water in company with natural ones. I again use dirty primrose silk and two pale yellow or pale grey hackles. I don't bother with a wing; but find that two hackles make a fly float much better than one. I always fish with two dry flies, one as a dropper about a foot above the tail fly. This helps me to see the flies in quick broken water and it increases the chance of covering a fish.

Ever since I was a small boy, on holiday in Skye, listening in the still night to the trickle of a stream or the roar of a spate, I have wished for a house of my own where from my room I could hear a river running. Now we have one.

After dinner on a calm summer evening it is only fifty yards from the front door, through the garden, to the river side. If the trout are rising it takes a matter of minutes to pick up a rod and slip on a pair of gum-boots. When the light begins to fade I like to fish water which is flowing but smooth. There is a glide immediately above a cauld below the house, which is just right, so I usually make my way there through alternate patches of warm and cooling air, while the birds are singing their evening songs. A few trout rise at first, and then they really start with rings forming and fading all over the smooth surface. At first you can see your flies; but later you must guess where they are and strike when you see a rise which may be at you. You may not catch many but it is the nicest way I know of spending that hour before bed-time.

Small rivers and streams have a fascination all of their own. You get to know each rock, every tree, and the way the water runs. After the winter floods you notice every change in their course.

Large rivers like the Tweed are very different. There is something majestic but impersonal about a great volume of water for ever flowing towards the sea. The trout are indeed much larger, but they are not nearly as good to eat. Some years the Tweed trout are almost inedible, which is a great pity and seriously detracts from one's pleasure in catching them. I think this may be due partly to over-stocking. There are a great many salmon parr and smolts competing for the available food. It takes a long time for the trout to get into condition.

If you stand by a run in the spring, when a good rise comes on, you will see what a tremendous number of trout there are in such a river. You can stay in one spot and have a dozen good trout rising in easy reach, and it is like this all over the river. On these occasions it is difficult to pick out one trout and fish for it, as they move about when they are taking in fairly deep water. They remain in one place far more when they are in shallow water. But they will all be 10 ins. to 14 ins. trout with an occasional larger one. You can stand quite still, with the water up to your knees, and catch as many as you want while they are rising well; on these occasions a landing net and a bag are an asset so that you don't have to go ashore each time you hook a fish.

To pick up an occasional trout before and after the rise you do have to move about, but not nearly as much as on a small stream. Select one run and fish it systematically, either with a wet fly working down the run, or a dry fly fishing up. You can fish your wet flies up-stream; but if you do you have to cast far more often, concentrate harder, and you cover and rise less fish—although, if you are looking, you will hook a higher percentage of the ones that rise to you.

As in a small river, you must know the most rewarding places to fish if you want to catch many trout. Exactly the same principles apply. You should fish the places where the water is not too deep and the speed right. Choose different places depending on the height of the river, and try to fish where catchable fish are rising.

The tail of a large pool, where the water accelerates over rounded stones before slipping over into the next pool, is another place to remember in a big river. If there is an upstream wind and consequently a ripple you need hardly fish anywhere else. Before the main rise starts a nymph or wet fly fished up and across and allowed to drag slightly before casting again is deadly. You probably won't see the rise, your line just stops; but if you then tighten you may have a fat and indignant trout kicking at the other end. Often the best fish in the river feed in such a place and you may easily catch a fish of 1 lb. or 1½ lb. Fish right on down to where the water appears to be running too fast, just above where it breaks, and you will still rise trout. Then, when the proper rise comes on, you should turn round and fish your dry-flies up the stream again. You hardly have to move at all to catch trout just as quickly as you can play and land them. These glides are usually a uniform depth, and rather than wading on upstream, you often do better to wade further across if you want to cover other fish; by so doing you can continue to fish in water flowing at your favourite speed. When you hook a fish he comes straight down towards you and does not disturb the other trout immediately above him. If you can recover line quickly enough to keep him near the surface you may be able to net him as he goes by, but don't crouch down in order to reach further with the landing-net, or the water will run in at the back of your waders.

Besides the rivers and streams of the valleys, the Border country has other waters to fish high up in the hollows among the hills. Here there is a number of lochs, each one different in character. Many have quantities of small trout but some have the opposite and preferable combination, a small number of large trout. The one which I and a few friends fish is intermediate in character. There are plenty of trout, but they average nearly ¾lb. The numbers present in any loch depend on the length of the spawning burns and the size depends on the number of fish competing for the available food. The spawning stream running into the one we fish is only a few hundred yards long and this produces enough but not too many trout. The food is plentiful.

Hill lochs have a great fascination. In winter they are often frozen and snow-covered; but in spring lambs are born to the blackfaced sheep grazing the coarse grass at the water's edge, curlews return to breed and fill the air with their nostalgic spring call, herons also nest in an adjacent fir wood, where they utter their raucous cries. There is not a human habitation in sight and not a human being, apart from the poachers one often finds when one arrives. They come out from the local town and walk a mile or so over the hill to reach the loch. At the moment the loch is rather overstocked so they do little harm, and as long as they disappear when I arrive I don't mind, but I get angry if they stop and argue for we have paid a rent and they haven't. I became really angry last year when I found that someone had broken into the boathouse and then fixed it so that I couldn't get in myself. There is nothing more infuriating than having to break one's own door.

The fish rise well from mid-April when they begin to get in condition. At first the rise is during the day and you can fish from the bank before the weeds grow. Later on in May and June there is a good rise in the evenings when the weather is fine and warm, but again if it is cold and wild they rise better through the day. I am told that it fishes well in the early morning; this time of day, however, I am quite prepared to leave to the poachers, and good luck to them.

It is interesting to study the pattern of a rise by watching fish rise naturally. You see an odd rise at first, then a number rise quite hard for five or ten minutes and then they go off again. After half an hour or so this may be repeated. Sometimes the rise reaches a climax, and every trout in the loch appears to be rising madly, then they gradually go off again. When they are all rising they can be almost impossible to catch: frantically you change your flies, thinking that you are missing the opportunity of a lifetime, and that you will fill the boat with fish if only you can find the fly they are taking. Finally, when they are clearly going off the take, you hook one, and say to yourself, 'If only I had tried that fly earlier!' Actually changing the fly probably had nothing to do with catching one. When the mad rise is on there are so many flies on the water that yours is outnumbered a hundred to one and those are the odds against rising a fish, but when the numbers of natural flies decrease your odds improve until you eventually rise one. All of us who fish the loch are experienced fishermen and women. We all catch trout. We all use different patterns and sizes of flies at the same time of year and under given conditions, and we swear by them!

The ones I use are a small Greenwell's, a Cinnamon and Gold and a Blue and Black. This last I find the best of all.

It looks just like the flies that often hatch in such pro-
fusion. I tie mine on a very small hook, with a black silk
body, a black hackle and starling wing.

Sometimes trout seem to take best a fly fished deep and
slowly, sometimes they prefer them nearer the surface
and moving quite fast. They may be in a mood to take
hard and be easy to hook, or they may just give your
fly a tweak and be impossible to hook. I don't think you
should be too quick on the strike when you see a trout rise
to your fly. If you give him time to turn and go down
before tightening, you increase the chance of hooking him.

It is most exciting when they begin rising within reach.
You must select a fish and cast over him at once, after
deciding which way he is going so that you can land your
fly on his nose. On some days most of the fish you cover will
rise to you, on others they completely ignore your efforts
but go on rising quietly to themselves. If it is the uncertainty of fishing that appeals to you I recommend a hill
loch, for of all the unpredictable fish these trout are in
a class of their own. The only advice I would offer is to
have two rods in the boat; one with a sinking line and one
with a floating one, and if you are fishing on a windy day
concentrate on the downwind end of the loch where the
flies will be blown and the fish will follow them.

Sometimes the conditions appear perfect, and for some
unknown reason no flies hatch and no trout rise. All you
can do on these occasions is to exhort the fish to bestir
themselves with the line from the Hymn which is clearly
applicable, 'Cast off dull sloth and joyful rise'.

When the fish are rising but in an awkward mood I am
just as happy at the oars, from which position I can
criticise the efforts of my friend who is fishing until
eventually he makes me change over with a, 'Well, just
see if you can do any better then.'

Bob and I have great fun fishing together. We sometimes
take our supper up to the loch on a fine evening. It usually
consists of pork pies, sticky cakes and gin. The last item

helps the fisherman and boatman to relax and enjoy themselves. It gets cold when the sun sets behind the hills and
the light fades from a pale sky, and you are glad of that
extra woolly. On a good calm night we expect to catch
about ten trout all between ½lb. and 1lb. They are excellent eating when in condition; about half have pink flesh
and half are a creamy white. They are great fighters and
you have to hold them hard to keep them out of the weeds.
When it is too dark to see a rise we go home down the
rough track that eventually leads to the road.

On one memorable night I broke the car's clutch rod on
a rock and had to drive home 15 miles without the use
of a clutch. It was impossible to start going uphill and
somewhat noisy changing gears. We did all right until we
met some traffic lights on an uphill slope and had to pass
all the cars that were waiting patiently for them to turn
green. Fortunately no car was coming the other way and
no policeman was around. The gear-box was never quite
the same again.

4

FLY-FISHING FOR SALMON

THERE ARE MANY recent developments in ways of fishing for salmon with what are called flies. Some of these new methods may endanger the lives of salmon, but others will definitely protect them. I can see no point in reducing one's chance of catching a fish by employing a method of angling which will do just that. But if you don't mind how few fish you catch, and enjoy making things more difficult for yourself than they already are, by all means fish by any method you please. Don't complain however, if you fish with a dry fly or greased line when the water temperature is 38°F. and catch nothing.

You can now fish a fly at any depth from an inch above the surface to several feet below it. Starting at the top, a number of salmon are caught on Highland lochs each year, using a blowline and a fly which hardly touches the surface. You can fish a floating dry fly upstream without drag, as for trout, or you can fish a large hairy fly downstream with half of it out of the water, which must look like a frantic mouse. Some people are successful with a smaller fly which just breaks or cuts the surface of the water. For fishing immediately below the surface there is the greased line method.

To present a fly to salmon in any of these ways you need a line which has been greased and floats on the surface, or an Air Cel line which floats in orjust below the surface of the water. A greased line keeps the fly a fraction higher in the water than does an Air Cel line.

If you wish the fly to sink a little there is an Air Cel line with an end portion which sinks. Finally there are all grades of Wet Cel lines which sink the fly deeper and deeper. If you aren't content with that, and want to scrape the bottom of the river, you can put a Jardine lead on the cast, and fish with lead wire wrapped round and round the fly. The use of lead makes casting difficult and even hazardous in a strong wind.

Last autumn a friend of mine, who is a large man, whacked himself on the back of the head with a particularly heavy fly and was rendered unconscious. Fortunately for him he landed in the bottom of the boat, for there was nobody else on board to rescue him from a watery grave. There was a full gale blowing, which made rowing impossible and the boatman was on the bank, holding the boat with a rope. The good boatman was much alarmed thinking Jock might have taken 'a shock', to use a local expression. He pulled him in to the shore with all his might. Jock's friends were, I fear, much amused when they heard about it afterwards.

There has always been a frightening selection of flies with which to fish; but in recent years vast numbers of new creations have flooded the market. Few of them actually represent any known beastie, and most are creatures of the imagination of the people who first make them. The influence of science fiction or surrealism has clearly been at work in some recent instances.

Displayed in shops you will find dry flies, wet flies, tube flies, hair flies: fat ones, thin ones, bright ones, dark ones; great big ones, and little tiny ones. There are flies with long shanks, or short shanks; of heavy or light metal, with one, two or three hooks.

Those who disapprove of treble hooks have coined the sinister name 'gang hooks' to denote their displeasure; their use is banned on some rivers.

I do not claim to have given all these methods a fair and extended trial, or to have caught salmon by them all, but

I know about most of them and have tried many. If you are experienced you know what you want and can ignore everything else. Even if you are a beginner don't be too alarmed. There is no need to buy several sizes of each pattern. There *is* a path through this seemingly impenetrable jungle, which I shall indicate when I have dealt briefly with the problem of getting the fly on to the water.

There is considerable choice of rods. You can get a microscopic one from America, or unearth a mammoth 18ft. pole from a dank castle in the Highlands, where the lairds of old used them to limber up before tossing the caber. They may still be found in gun-rooms propped up against deer's antlers. I know, because one was produced recently for a Salmon and Trout Association casting competition near Perth. Everyone who tried it cast flies farther than they ever had before, until it broke in half.

I recommend a 14ft. fibreglass rod made by Farlow's. They are comparatively inexpensive, extremely strong and very light. Their action is like that of a greenheart. A light hold on the handle and correct timing is all important. You can cast as heavy a line and fly with them as ever you need, or a light line and fly in the summer. But it is nice to have a light split-cane rod for use at that time of year; if you get one with good action there is nothing more pleasant to fish with. The action of rods varies enormously, and it is most important to have the advice of an expert, and I don't mean the salesman, when making a choice.

If you can cast a fly with a trout rod you can quickly learn how to do so with a double-handed salmon rod, but expert tuition is always of value. There is, however, another way of casting a salmon fly which takes some mastering.

During the last casting competition for which I entered at a game fair, I managed to break a brand new £30 split cane rod, lent by a famous firm of rod makers. At the time I was trying to Spey cast into a hoop. After this remarkably good half-crown's worth, not wanting to repeat the performance later with my own rod, I went and had a lesson in how to Spey cast. On many rivers, particularly in a high water, you often have to throw a long line from a bank where the trees grow close by the water's edge. For this the Spey cast is essential. Captain Edwards corrected some of my worst mistakes in his own forceful and inimitable way in about five minutes. I can remember each one of them.

Unfortunately the practical fisherman is apt to be put off by the artificial conditions of a casting competition. There is always a wooden platform to fish from. It is so easy to coil line or nylon on a smooth surface before shooting them at the end of your forward cast. It is a different matter if you are standing on a bank covered in thistles, or wading in a swift river, yet there are very few of us practical fishermen who do not benefit by instruction from an expert. The last time I stood peering over the ropes at the experts in action in a competition I was struck by two thoughts: how lucky they were always to have the wind behind them when making their long casts, and what fun it would be if one could get on to their platform unobserved with a tin of treacle to spread it on the floor.

It is rather more difficult to become a good fly caster than an adequate bait caster. Some people get the hang of it more easily than others, and youth is an advantage in this respect. But an elderly novice can catch a salmon on a fly in a surprisingly short time, given the built-in luck which attends all novices at fishing. Last autumn one luckless Tweed salmon took a fly which was almost touching the bank and only 5 yards from the point of the rod: this being as far as the boy could cast it. Meanwhile, on the same beat two experts were throwing lines about 25 yards long all day. Neither of them had a touch.

When you have mastered casting, how and with what fly are you going to fish? If you have a boatman or gillie you will do as you are told; if not, you will have to make up your own mind. There is one rule with which some fishermen, and more important most salmon, will agree. When the water is cold and big, fish deep with a large fly. When it is warm, fish near the surface with a smaller fly. The critical temperature is around 50°F. In this country this temperature is usually reached about the end of April; day and night temperatures don't vary much. In Iceland they do: as the sun sets and goes off the river, the water temperature falls rapidly. When the water passes the critical temperature fish will no longer take a fly near the surface; they will however take a deeply sunken fly very well. So fish a sunk fly in spring and autumn and one near the surface in summer.

If it is warm weather, and you have a well-stocked beat to fish, which method of fishing a surface fly should you use? You may want to catch a salmon rather badly, because an aged and wealthy relative is coming to dinner, in which case discard any thought of fishing with a floating dry fly right from the start. To use one would seriously jeopardise any chance of serving fresh salmon steaks for supper. Salmon have been caught on a dry fly in this country, but only after prolonged effort by experts and on very good beats. The Americans are the experts in this form of fishing, but it appears that in their own continent they go fishing with a somewhat different end in view from the one most of us have over here. They fish purely for the sport and put nearly all the salmon they catch back in the river; we like to see ours lying on the bank, preferably in a row. That dinner party would not be the same success if you regaled the aged relative with tales of the salmon you had caught and returned while he sank his dentures into a piece of boiled cod.

Salmon will often take a small fly near the surface, swimming through the water at an even speed, more eagerly than anything else you can offer them, preferring this to all the baits fished with a spinning rod. The method is known as 'greased line fishing'. One day it may become unfashionable with anglers but I don't think it ever will with salmon. The fly is cast in the normal way across and slightly down the stream, and left in the water until the action of the current brings it round below the fisherman. It is kept near the surface by a floating line. Few people still use grease to make a line float since the advent of the Air Cel line, which floats just in the surface, and keeps the fly at a depth of 3ins. to 8ins., depending on the length of the cast and the strength of the current.

Grease has disadvantages. It has to be frequently and thickly applied to make a salmon line float. This stops the line shooting so well. The grease also gets on the cast which then won't sink, so that the fly skates on the surface. It isn't supposed to, although fish sometimes take when it is doing this. But grease also has one advantage. You nearly always see a fish rise to the fly because the line is on, and the fly so near the surface. I don't see as many rises using an Air Cel line, but nevertheless I prefer an Air Cel line for salmon and a greased line for trout.

Much has been written about greased line fishing, but there are still some points that need clearing up. One of the practices recommended is the 'mending' of the line. This is rolling a loop of line up or down stream while the fly is fishing the pool. A fly swimming through the water at an even speed can be most attractive to salmon, but if it gives a sudden convulsive jerk when a fish is following it, he will turn away and take no further interest. You are supposed to be able to mend your line without moving the fly, but I have never met the man who can always do so. With an Air Cel line it is even more difficult.

The practical and experienced fishermen I have watched occasionally make one mend just as the line lands on the water. If there is a strong current in the centre of a pool, and you want to retard the speed of the fly as it swims through it, an upstream mend will achieve this. As for mending the line downstream there is no possible point to it except when fishing a very narrow river. This accelerates the motion of the fly through the water, and there is a much easier way of doing this, which is by pulling the line in by hand.

There is another point which may perplex you as it does me. How can you cast down and across the stream, and fish the fly round to your bank without 'drag'? You can't if the words means the same to us both. I define drag as any unnatural motion imparted to a fly due to its attachment to line and cast. It has also been said and oft repeated that the fly should float down 'like a dead leaf'. When have you seen a leaf, dead or alive, swim below the surface from one side of the current to the other? Every trout fisher knows that it is only possible to avoid drag by fishing upstream. It is the controlled motion imparted by the 'drag' from the line which attracts the salmon.

Many salmon fishermen, whether fishing a surface or a deep fly, always rely entirely on the current to bring the fly round. After casting they just wait until the fly is below them before taking a step downstream and casting again.

On days when salmon are taking a fly, very frequently all the offers come when you are fishing the same kind of water—it may be in the fast streams, smooth glides or still pools. Other types of water, which are holding just as many fish, yield nothing. This, I think, is often accounted for by the speed at which the fly is moving through the water. Fishermen are always ready to change a fly, and pattern and size can make a difference. But how many try varying the speed of the fly through the water?

When you fish with a fly you must be imitating something that the salmon thinks is edible or a nuisance, but certainly it is something he has seen before. A fly hardly ever represents any fly that ever flew. It is really a lure just as much as spoons, minnows and plugs are lures. When you select a pattern from your fly tin you don't know what you are imitating unless you select a specific fly like a Shrimp Fly or a March Brown.

However good a beat you are fishing, and on whatever

famous river, be sure you will have plenty of time for contemplation. Frequently you will wonder why the countless fish you are covering so expertly won't take anything you can offer them. Then I hope you will have cause to ask why that particular one suddenly did take.

One thing worth considering is the nature of the sea, for this was where the salmon you are trying to interest recently fed voraciously. Even here he didn't feed all the time; there were periods of feeding followed by periods of resting and digestion. The sea is a vast place and there are countless thousands of things for salmon to eat in it, nobody knows how many. They must vary from place to place and with the time of year. We can't know what they ate on the route home from Greenland; but we may understand something of the last things they ate in or near the river estuary. The numbers of shrimps and prawns and small fry vary from estuary to estuary and indeed from year to year, and this probably accounts for the preference of salmon in different rivers for different flies and baits.

Your fly is likely to succeed if it resembles something the fish have recently been eating, and, perhaps, if you are fishing at the time of day when they were accustomed to feed. Even in fresh water salmon sometimes take and swallow food into their stomachs. This I call feeding even although they can't digest it. Salmon certainly retain the urge to take things that look like the food they have recently been eating, even if they usually spit them out again. Gradually this urge fades and becomes less frequent, so that fresh run fish are much easier to catch than stale ones which have been in the river a long time. In some years and on some rivers a shrimp fly is most effective, on other occasions fish take different flies in preference. A fly that resembled an elver was most effective in an Icelandic river, but on English rivers it is frequently useless.

Each and every different thing that the salmon eats in the sea will move with a different action and at a different speed. It is well worth studying every small creature you see in an estuary, from a boat, or when bathing, and so form a picture of the sort of movements you should try to copy. Even if you don't know what you are imitating it must be right to vary the speeds and actions of your flies and baits.

If you are fishing a slow pool on the Tweed the boatman often starts at the bottom and works the boat slowly up stream, and this imparts a little more speed to the fly. It really is much simpler to give motion to a fly by pulling your line in by hand. Indeed if you are fishing loggy water from the bank, or when wading, it is the only way of bringing your fly round at all. You certainly don't want to walk backwards. There is a number of ways by which you can pull in line. You can use short quick pulls with the hand that isn't holding the rod, catching the line with the index finger of the rod hand as you reach for more line; or you can take long slow pulls. It doesn't matter how you do it. Develop a way that suits you and then keep varying the speeds. If you haven't previously done this try it out, but don't expect immediate or startling results—salmon fishing isn't usually like that. If you are to continue as a salmon fisherman you mustn't be easily discouraged, and you should keep trying new methods.

A few years ago we gave a day's fishing to a man who didn't know the beat, so I went down for a while to show him where to fish and to row the boat for him. It had been a disappointing spring and we had caught few fish. The river was low and the only place where there were any salmon was a deep pool with hardly any current. There was an easterly gale blowing upstream and a big wave on this pool. It looked to me a good chance if we could get it fished, but it was clearly quite impossible to fish in the normal way, starting at the top of the pool and casting down and across the river into that gale. The angler wasn't very experienced and couldn't nearly cast into such a wind. He could cast slightly across it and land the fly well upstream of the boat and about fifteen yards away. I had to row the boat with the bows pointing downstream, starting at the bottom of the pool and gradually ease it upstream. I told him to cast as best he could and pull the fly in until it was quite close to the boat. The loose line became entangled in the bottom of the boat, and it took several casts for him to get it all out again. This is rather awkward when you first try, but you soon get quick at it.

He had only had about ten decent casts and the fly was within ten yards of the boat when the line went tight and there was a flash of silver through a wave. Away went the fish, fortunately followed by the line. With lots of loose line in the bottom of the boat it is very easy to get it caught round a toe or a floor-board, which causes immediate disaster. He was thrilled and I was fully occupied with rowing the boat into the wind. He didn't pull it very hard, and there was an enormous 'belly' in the line between the rod top and where it entered the water. I tried to keep him in fairly close contact with the fish. However, all went well and it was duly landed and admired. He hooked another shortly afterwards, but unfortunately it got round a rock and broke him. It was entirely my fault as I had the boat too far from the fish, which would have been inexcusable in normal conditions, but there was a great gust of wind and I had to row as hard as I could to stay in the same place.

We have caught many fish from this pool when there has been hardly any current. You always have to pull the line in by hand.

There was a wonderful pool in a river in Iceland, where the salmon took as we all dream they may one day. There was a slight current under the far bank. The rest of the pool was still water but full of willing salmon. You had to pull the line in by hand after the fly left the current, and if you did the results were spectacular. If they missed the first time they usually had a second go. I had a ciné camera one day when Brenda was fishing. She had caught one and was fishing away again when she said, 'One rose at it', so

I focused the camera on the rod top. Two seconds later the top bent and she raised the rod and hooked the fish. The film came out rather well and is a great tribute to the enthusiasm of Icelandic salmon for taking flies.

The drawback to fishing a river like that is you expect British salmon to behave in the same way when you return. Gradually you realise that they never do.

There is nothing in the fisherman's world that gives a bigger thrill than seeing a salmon coming up to a surface fly. There is a bulge in the water, then a swirl as he turns, an agonising second's wait until you see if he has the fly in his mouth; then, if he has, the line draws away. He has done his stuff. He has survived the hazards of several years at sea and travelled a long way to take your hook into his mouth. Now is the chance to make certain of cold salmon for lunch on Sunday. The question is what are you going to do about it? The next move is up to you. There are several alternatives. You can hold on to everything and strike like a maniac, or pull line off the reel and let everything go slack; just hang on and hope, or wade ashore, walk twenty yards downstream and then see whether he is still holding on. Different fishermen do and recommend others to do all these things. The most popular and widely supported action is to do absolutely nothing at all, merely to hold on and wait until there is a hard tug, then raise the rod and let the reel turn. To take no action is usually easier than it sounds, because after hours, days, or even weeks of fishing completely blank, the very last thing you are expecting is for a salmon to take, so you almost certainly won't be looking. If by chance you are looking you must not strike or even twitch the fly when you see a movement. It is usually the salmon approaching, about to open his mouth, and if you move the fly he will miss it. Apparently the Grimersta is an exception to this, and there you must strike at once to hook the fish.

Salmon take flies in different ways depending on the

place, water speed and temperature. They also take the fly into their mouths for different lengths of time depending on their mood. A fish can pick it up for a second and spit it out again as readily as a schoolboy can spit out a cherry stone. Or he may hold on to it for several seconds. The advice about letting line go, so that the current carries it below the fish and the fly is drawn into the corner of the fish's mouth or 'scissors', is fine if the fish holds on long enough. I reckon that for every fish that does this about three spit the fly out before they are hooked. It may work in a strong current; it can't if there is very little.

Every trout fisher knows what happens when a trout takes an artificial fly. He keeps it in his mouth until it reaches the sensitive nerves of the mouth and tongue, which inform him that it isn't the real thing, then he immediately expels it. The angler must strike after the fish has taken it well into his mouth, and before he spits it out again. The same often happens with salmon. They were all parr once and took real flies. Now they are adult they don't even want to swallow the fly, so are even more likely to expel it than trout.

Once the salmon has your fly in his mouth and you feel this, or see your line moving away, I think you should do something positive. You can't strike as you do with a trout rod. With a two-handed salmon rod a controlled strike would be almost impossible, for, remember, the first action of the rod tip is down and then sharply up. If you raise your rod point slowly you gradually increase the pressure on the fly and this can alarm the fish without hooking it, just as a strike which is timed right but is too gentle will fail to hook a trout.

Unless the point of the hook is needle sharp and engaged, a salmon will spit it out. If I were holding a hook firmly in my hand and you pulled it, gradually increasing the pressure, I could let it go without being hooked. But if you gave it a sharp jerk you would hook me. Rods are designed to prevent any sharp jerk once they are bent. It needs considerable force to make a heavy hook penetrate a salmon's hard mouth and it must be administered fairly quickly. I think the best action is to keep the rod pointing directly at the fish, and hold tightly on to the line by hand. In a fast current the line will go very tight when a fish takes and it may be best to hold the rod up a little. You must let go of the line as soon as it is tight enough to hook the fish and before it is pulled hard enough to break the nylon. Find out how much strain is needed to pull the hook you are using into a fish's mouth, and make sure the nylon is strong enough with a good margin of safety.

In a slack current the fish may not pull hard enough to hook himself. Then, still pointing your rod directly at the fish, pull in line firmly and immediately by hand until you judge that it is tight enough to hook him. With a big fly and strong nylon pull him right to the surface and let him kick about for a bit. He may get off at once, but then he would have anyway. A pool where fish hook themselves in a high water may become too still for this to happen when the water falls in. If you then find you are missing fish, start pulling the line in by hand when you feel a fish take.

I claim no originality for this advice. Mr Pashley, one of the greatest of all anglers on the Wye, did this. You won't often hook a fish in the 'scissors', but there are lots of other good holds for a fly in a fish's mouth. I am sure you hook many fish in this way which you would not have done otherwise.

If a fish takes when you are hand-lining, particularly with large flies and a sunk line in the autumn, go on pulling in by hand until the line is good and tight. Then you can raise the rod and begin playing the fish.

Whatever you may do when a salmon takes your fly, the hook is of the utmost importance. It is the cheapest part of all your equipment and I suppose for this reason has recently received little consideration. Hooks are now far less reliable than they were twenty-five years ago. They are still identical in design to the ones found in prehistoric anglers' tombs in the Middle East and quite possibly inferior in strength. But any criticism of the tackle industry in this respect receives nothing but a rude letter. The only new design in hooks that I have seen recently comes from Holland; these have needle sharp points turned outwards. In practically all hooks the point is parallel with the shank. You can get outpoint ones in this country from Dickson's in Edinburgh, and they are far better at hooking and holding salmon. Single, double or treble hooks should all have their points directed slightly outwards if the pull on the cast is to drive them home with the greatest ease.

If you use tube flies there is no reason to put on a larger treble just because you are using a longer tube. The tendency to do so is a hangover from the days when a large fly had a large hook. There must be an optimum size of hook for each size of fish, something small enough to go into his mouth easily and fine enough not to require too hard a pull to make it penetrate; but large enough to take a good hold and strong enough not to break under reasonable strain. You must use a heavier metal with a thick heavy fly line, which is difficult to drag through the water. A fish running fast and deep up the far side of a really strong stream will exert great pressure on the cast and hook. He will snap 12lb. nylon with the greatest ease, although the strain at your rod top may only be 1lb., and will break or bend a hook made of too light metal.

But whatever hooks you use, one thing is absolutely certain—they must be sharp. Hooks arrive from the makers, coloured black or brown with a protective paint or varnish. You must remove every spot of it from the point of the hook or it can't be really sharp and a hook must be so sharp that it won't pull over the end of your finger when held by the nylon. A fish's mouth is a hard and slippery place and his jaw is very powerful. If the hook point is sharp enough to catch in the mucous-membrane lining the mouth he will have far more difficulty in getting rid of a hook once it is in his mouth. You will in consequence hook more of the fish that touch the fly, and lose about one in eight instead of one in three.

There are many warm weather days when salmon should, but for some reason do not, take a greased line fly. Then there is nothing to be lost by trying out something different. I fancy the large mouse-like tube fly, fished half out of the water on a very short line; but I have only tried it in the autumn when the temperature was far too low. I am sure it would work in a quick, narrow stream. I have found mice in sea-trout and brown trout. Another thing I intend trying is a dapping fly with an upstream wind. Trout flies are often blown to the top of a pool in these conditions, and trout congregate right in the quick water and take like mad. I don't see why a dapping fly continually bobbing over a salmon's nose shouldn't remind him of his days as a parr and goad him into action. There is far more movement in a dapping fly than a dry fly, and I believe that it would be more attractive as a consequence, but the number of times you could use it would be limited by the wind.

Part of the fun of salmon fishing is trying out new ideas, and there is plenty of scope for everyone to try out his own. Only the fringe of the possibilities has so far been explored. Even if your innovations are not successful at once there is always tomorrow when you may discover that irrisistable something the salmon are all waiting for. Anyway it is much more fun trying something new than flogging away with the same old flies in the same old way, even if the results are identical.

There are conditions in the summer when one considers fishing with a sunk fly in preference to one on the surface. The classical directions for greased line fishing say you should fish a floating line when the air is warmer than the water, and a sinking line if the air is colder than the water. I find this is often wrong, and you should be guided only by the water temperature. Often in May, when the water temperature has been over 50°F., I have arrived on the river bank to find a bitterly cold north-east wind blowing and the air temperature about 42°F. These are excellent conditions for catching salmon on a greased line, perhaps the best of all. There is usually a great trout rise too.

Then consider a small dirty flood in June when there has been a thunder storm in the hills. I once arrived to fish the Tweed equipped only with greased line tackle and found the water so thick that I couldn't see my feet when wading up to my knees. The water temperature was right for greased line fishing; but it seemed impossible that a salmon near the bottom could see a fly near the surface. I wished that I had a sinking line with me, as it appeared to offer the only slight chance of catching a fish. I put on the largest fly I had in the tin which holds my small flies, and started fishing without hope. I caught one and had three other pulls in the first pool. Just for interest and in order to have a better chance of hooking the fish I tried a much smaller fly, a normal size for June. During the rest of the day I had five more rises and caught three more fish. The river was still as dirty at the end of they day as it was at the beginning. A mistake we often make is to imagine that animals' minds and sensory organs are the same as ours. They are not, and fish can see through muddy water much better than one thinks. These fish were all lying in 4 to 5ft. of water and the fly was 2ins. below the surface.

Bait fishing on the Tweed ends on September 15th, and it is with a feeling of relief that one puts away all the paraphernalia of spinning. Another nice thing is that one may no longer sell the fish one catches. Fishmongers must make way for sportsmen, and rents are consequently more reasonable. All your tackle now goes into one pocket and there is not that haunting feeling that some totally different bait may be luring countless salmon to some other angler's rod.

October is so often a lovely month; the water clear and the bottom clean and sparkling after a September flood: bright, frosty nights and warm sunny days. The autumn colouring of the trees and the blue of the sky is reflected in the still pools. It is a great joy to be alive and breathe the cold clean air.

When you arrive at the selected pool you often see a fish show before you even start fishing. The sight of a fresh run salmon will even take your mind from the beauties of the scene. As you wade out and start fishing, hope and excitement are superimposed on your feelings of joy. The easy action of a rod is a pleasure; the line shoots straight and falls on the water, with a little splash from the fly beyond. Down there among the rocks the salmon are balanced on the current, and quite soon you may see the line draw away and feel it go tight. At first you can't believe that it is a fish, it feels so heavy and motionless; but then comes the heavy deliberate tug-tug of a large and, you hope, well-hooked salmon, and a flash of silver—yards long it appears—in the clear water. This is the moment. During the next ten minutes you will go through agonies of hope and fear which never lessen with age. When you have landed a fresh run 20lb. salmon you have something that is as aesthetically beautiful as anything can be, perfect in every respect. But you must eventually take your eyes from it. You did not think the surroundings of trees and river could be any more beautiful than they were when you started fishing. Now they are.

The autumn run varies from year to year, but recently there have been countless thousands of fresh autumn fish running up the Tweed. They will spawn shortly, but they are as bright as springers and covered with sea lice. Many are large fish, and each year several over 30lb. are caught. By November the river is often high and sometimes coloured, so a large fly fished deep is the answer. Nowadays practically everyone uses a tube fly and I am rather sorry for Mr Parker who invented the things and receives no royalties.

1   My place is the Island of Skye

2   Camasunary

Tube flies are absurdly easy to make, and anyone whose fingers are sufficiently nimble to sew on a button need never buy another. All you need is a dyed deer's tail from a tackle shop, a pair of scissors, some wax and the reel of silk you sew buttons on with. Visit your electrician and get a few feet of medium rubber-covered flex, black, red or any colour you fancy. Cut off as long a piece as you wish and pull it off the wire. There is the tube. These rubber tubes are rather light and split rather easily, so it is best to whip the ends, but they cost virtually nothing. You can buy aluminium tubes with plastic linings, which prevent the nylon from fraying on the metal; they are also light, and to make them sink you can wrap lead wire round them or coat them with plastic metal or solder as I do. When they are dry I paint them black or red, or I leave them silvery. There is no point in making the tube fly too heavy. As long as it sinks at the same speed as the line, that is all that is required. A heavy fly is much more difficult to cast and a great strain on the nylon. To make the fly, cut off a small bunch of hair, hold the cut end against one end of your tube and tie it there with the well waxed silk. Then apply your wife's or girl friend's nail varnish to the whipping. You need no vice and it takes less time than to sew on that button. You only need two colours of hair; yellow and orange in varying lengths. But if you want variation you can always take a snip with your scissors at a passing dog or teenage boy.

It is important to get the fly well down in big cold waters, so use the appropriate lines. Never use nylon of less than 20lb. breaking strain. Even in the summer there is no need to fish lighter than 10lb. nylon. It is invisible and there is little evidence that salmon are gut-shy anyway. Breaking in fish is inexcusable as it is usually avoidable; but, mark you, we all do it through carelessness. One should always re-tie a fly to the nylon after playing a fish because knots in nylon pull tighter and tighter until they eventually break with very little strain. It is advisable to

c

put on a new cast after catching two or three fish or after any undue strain, such as a fish getting round a snag while being played. Nylon is so reliable that one tends to become careless, but don't then blame the nylon if you lose a fish.

However well you may fish something far more important is essential before you catch salmon. You must be lucky. Luck comes and goes but when yours is in, play it hard, because be sure the day won't be far off when it will desert you to alight on some less worthy mortal. When it is truly out stay at home, for the few fish you hook will all get off.

During the third week of October there was an example of this. Bob and I were fishing a beat below Galashiels. Two adjacent pools were well stocked with fish. On both days he fished the lower while I fished the upper. On the first, in half an hour he caught three and had another pull while I never moved a fish. Two days later, at the same time of day, I caught four in the hour, the biggest 19lb., and he never had an offer. You can't do anything about it. It is no good changing pools; you must play the luck right out.

Whenever my luck temporarily deserts me and I begin moaning, I recall two occasions when it stood by me. The first was when I got out of a blazing Mosquito aircraft which I had just put into a very rough sea. The nearest I came to fishing for the next two seasons was to read a notice stating that for prisoners-of-war fishing was 'Verboten'.

The second was in connection with fishing and took place a few years afterwards.

After the war I lived in Yorkshire for some time. It is, as everybody knows, a wonderful sporting country with the best hunting and grouse shooting to be found anywhere; but it lacks one thing, a proper salmon river. I was a member of a club which had fishing on the Ure, but a salmon was very rarely caught except just below Aysgarth falls, and that in the late autumn. The beat where I could

fish was just below Masham, and nobody had caught a
salmon out of it since well before the war.

Yorkshire may not have a salmon river but it is famous
for its hospitality. One Sunday I was asked to lunch by a
family, where there was a very attractive girl, and they
lived not far from the river. I had just received a new 13ft.
salmon fly rod which I wanted to try out, so I took it
with me. I arrived in good time for a glass of what I knew
was excellent sherry, to find that both the parents were out
to lunch and the cook was away for the day. However
Brenda produced a first-class meal and the lightest Yorkshire pudding I had ever tasted.

It had been a dull, cloudy, June morning following
several wet days and after lunch it began to rain steadily
again. Under similar circumstances no foreigners would
have moved off the sofa and it did indeed provide a powerful attraction; but you really have to go out on Sunday
afternoon. We were terribly British and went salmon
fishing in a river where there was no hope of catching a
salmon.

We didn't see the river until we reached Masham, and
at the sight of it I nearly turned back. It was in a chocolate-coloured flood. I had caught fish on a bait with as
much colour in the water; but it seemed quite hopeless for
a fly even if there were fish in the river, which was most
unlikely. However, the real object was to try out the rod,
so we decided to go on and fish until it was time to go
back to tea.

We left the car on a cart track and put the rod up. To
the cast I attached the largest fly I had, a 5.0 Garry. It
was before the days of tube flies, so the hook was enormous
—more fitted for suspending the Sunday joint than
catching a salmon. I hadn't fished that particular beat
since before the war, and then only for trout, but I could
remember the pool that was reputed to hold salmon. It
was a walk of a mile and there was plenty of river nearer
where we could have tried out the rod; but it seemed

stupid, having come so far, to fish anywhere but the most likely spot. We had to go there just in case the incredible should have happened and a salmon had swum up the Humber, the Ouse, past Hull, through York and on the hundred odd miles from the sea to Masham.

Off we set under dripping trees and through soaking grass until we came to the wood where the pool lay. Clearly nobody had fished it for years. The nettles and willow-herb were as high as our heads, and bushes grew right down to the water's edge. I hardly recognised the place when we had fought our way through the under-growth and emerged on the river bank. It was a large round pool with a shingle bank on our side opposite the fairly narrow run in, which was about twenty yards long. Below this run the pool opened out with a backwater on our side overhung by trees whose branches touched the water. The current ran down the far side of the pool, which was rocky. In days gone by salmon were reputed to have lain and taken in the run at the head of the pool.

I was wearing thigh boots, so I went up above the run and waded a short way out into the river with great caution, for the water was so coloured that I couldn't see where I was putting my feet. It was much too coloured to see what depth of water I was fishing in, but I remem-bered that it deepened rapidly beyond the shingle bed. I started fishing with a short line in the shallow water and then took short steps and lengthened the line gradually to cover the deepening run thoroughly.

I was enjoying myself. The action of the rod was very nice. It was rather stiff, like a good dry fly rod, and made positive action on the part of the angler essential. It gave one great control over the fly and felt extremely powerful, like a great rod for casting a fly into a strong wind. Better still there was an extremely attractive girl sitting happily, if somewhat damp, on the bank waiting patiently for nothing to happen. In fact it was a typical British way of spending a Sunday afternoon.

I wasn't thinking of anything in particular when I felt quite a heavy and very distinct pull. It was a single pull not the *tug-tug* of a trout. It couldn't be a salmon but it was exactly what a salmon would have felt like. It was so impossible that my heart didn't even begin thumping.

'Something pulled it,' I said.

'Oh really?' she said politely.

'Might have been a trout,' I added.

'Probably was,' she said, not showing much excitement, and rightly.

I stood there for a moment and then waded ashore and went two yards back upstream leaving the same length of line out. After all it had felt like a salmon even if it couldn't have been one, so there was no harm in fishing over the spot again. I waited a moment longer and then started fishing again. One step another cast, one step another cast . . . The line shot out straight and the fly fell with a little plop in the broken coloured water on the far side of the stream. The loop of line from the rod tip to the water rose and fell with the motion of the rod. The fly swam through the coloured water with rhythmical movements. Then the loop of the line was gone as it drew tight. For a second it might have been a log, then there was that unmistakable tug. I raised the rod and felt the certain weight of a salmon. I just couldn't believe it for a moment. Then the fish went off down the stream pulling line from the reel, while I waded ashore. The impossible had happened. As full realisation of it struck me my excitement became such that I felt breathless and rather unwell. Then I remembered the girl.

'I've got one on,' I said.

'Oh really, what?'

'A salmon.'

She didn't show much excitement as she had never seen a salmon caught, but a second later a great tail broke the surface some thirty yards below us and she became as excited as I was. The fish played fairly steadily for a short time. I then realised that if I lost it nobody would begin to believe that I had ever hooked one, which is a terrible predicament for any angler to be in.

Suddenly it tore off to the tail of the pool, where I couldn't possibly follow because of the tree and deep backwater on my side of the river. I held on and hoped for the best, and after an agonising moment it came back up the pool again. It then made a series of short runs up and down the pool, but after a while it began to tire and came within a few yards of the bank.

We saw it very plainly, a fish of about 15lb.—too plainly. For to my horror I saw that it was hooked in the extreme tip of the upper jaw, with practically the whole fly projecting beyond its mouth. After showing me the desperate insecurity of the hold the fish went off again with a rush, straight under the overhanging tree and played deep down in the backwater where there were bound to be all sorts of horrors like tree stumps and bed-steads left by previous floods. The fact that they were invisible in the swirling brown water made it just that much worse. Then the line went solid and dead on a snag, but after an endless second it came clear again.

Gradually the fish came closer as it became tired. It wallowed in the shallows, then with an effort made short runs out into the stream again until the steady strain turned its head once more towards the bank. I felt that my heart was thumping audibly. The last few moments of playing a salmon are always the worst, and this was such a very special fish. So nearly safe, but would the hold give? It so often does at that last moment when the fish goes on its side. Without exerting an extra ounce of strain I waited until the fish came in and hadn't the strength to turn away again. There he was in a few inches of coloured water, turning slowly from side to side. Then he lay still. I didn't dare ask the girl to hold the rod in case anything went wrong and she might blame herself. So holding the rod in my left hand, I slowly approached, lent down and got my

hand round its tail and pushed it up the shingle. I had it!
I hadn't dared think I really would land that fish, and the
relief and delight were terrific. I expect I jumped up and
down and thumped the poor girl on the back, but all I can
remember is the wonderful feeling of having achieved an
angling impossibility. I shall never forget it, and whenever
I have a run of bad luck now I remember my fantastic luck
on this occasion with due gratitude. Besides, my luck on
this occasion wasn't entirely confined to catching the
salmon.

It was quite a clean fish of 17lb. and I was in a daze of
delight for quite a long time afterwards. I gave half the
fish to the girl, who most certainly deserved it. She was
already a good trout fisher and threw a nice line. Now she
has caught many salmon and sea trout. Her Yorkshire
pudding is as light as ever, and she has many quick and
excellent ways of cooking fish.

5

BAIT FOR SALMON

I. MINNOWS, SPRATS, PLUGS AND SPOONS

ON THE 15th February everyone fishing the Tweed throws down the fly rod with which he has been casting large tube flies and picks up his spinning rod. It is interesting to note the effect that this has on the numbers of fish caught. On a prolific beat it is possible to make a comparison which will indicate the effectiveness of fly against minnow. If rods on the best beats have been averaging 4 to 5 salmon a day on fly, the catch is likely to go up to 9 or 10 if conditions remain the same. This is usually temporary and catches drop back to the 5 or 6 mark after a day or two.

The fashion in spinning rods has changed recently. They used to be made of stiff split cane. Nowadays most people use fibreglass rods which are much shorter and more whippy. While a short rod is quite adequate for playing even the largest of salmon, it has its disadvantage when fishing. You cannot raise or lower the point so far to control the depth at which your bait fishes. Fishing from a boat this doesn't matter, but I don't like these mini-rods for fishing from the bank. A whippy rod is an advantage when you are using a fixed spool reel. I prefer a rather stiffer action for use with a multiplying reel. If the rod is whippy you can get your timing wrong when casting into a wind, and end up with an awful bird's nest of an over-run even with these almost fool-proof modern multiplying reels.

There is one thing you must watch with a fibre-glass spinning rod and that is the end ring. If this is an agate lined ring, one touch against a stone when casting will smash the agate and leave a sharp metal rim which will fray and cut your spinning line. If it is not of agate the line may wear a groove in the metal of the ring, which will also fray your line, especially under the pressure of playing a fish. This is a real danger which needs watching.

There are many makes of fixed spool and multiplying reels; most are perfectly adequate. It is a mistake to pay too little, but for the average fisherman there is little point in paying extra to have his name engraved on a gold plate on the side of the reel. The fish will never know. If possible try someone else's reel before deciding which kind to buy. The line on either must be monofilament nylon. It is so reliable, strong and inexpensive. It is better on a multiplier than braided nylon because it doesn't pick up as much water and consequently your hands don't become so wet. On a freezing day in early spring you don't want wet hands.

There is no point in using nylon of less than 10lb. or more than 20lb. breaking strain. Either is so fine that it offers very little resistance to the water. A fish can run deep up the far side of a strong stream and the strain at the fish end is not appreciably more than at the rod tip. For this reason you can afford to use treble hooks made of much lighter metal than when fishing with a heavy fly line. With these it is much easier to hook a fish and needs less of a pull. But remember that if your reel is fitted with a slipping clutch of any kind, and most are, you must have this adjusted tight enough to make sure it will pull the hook home over the barb. This will have to be varied depending on the size and metal thickness of your treble hook.

Finally you need a swivel to prevent the line kinking. There is usually one at the bait. One ball-bearing swivel two feet away is all you need. They are excellent if you make sure they are working correctly and I have only once had one break.

C*

It is extremely easy to learn to cast a bait adequately, but it takes a great deal of practice to develop real accuracy. This isn't essential although the man who fishes really accurately will catch the most fish. I have never dared enter for a bait-casting competition, because the more I concentrate on accuracy the more erratic I become. I am sure I make all sorts of mistakes yet I should be embarrassed by a lesson: I have done it so long and should be so much better at it. For a beginner I am sure a lesson from a real expert would be of great assistance.

By far the most intriguing problem of bait fishing is what bait to use and when. Tackle shops are filled with a bewildering array of every shape, size and colour of minnow, plug and spoon. Every time you go into a shop you will see something new, specially designed to catch the eye of the jaded angler if not of the salmon. The fisherman, faced with a new bait, and remembering his fruitless efforts in the past, mutters, 'By Jove, now that might just be the answer', and promptly buys it.

Besides the metal lures you will find bottles and jars full of natural little fish from all swims of life: sprats, gold, scarlet and silver; gudgeon, eel tails, natural minnows and prawns; shrimps and artificial worms. There is no end to the selection.

Fashions in baits change. For fishing in the early spring I have seen it go from the dyed golden sprat and natural silver sprat to the metal minnow and now to the Toby spoon. I really don't think one need often bother with natural baits in early spring. But I do like freshly caught minnows later on and a golden sprat is very showy in a coloured water. They are a nuisance to mount and need constant attention to see they are spinning properly. Then a kelt comes and chews them up and you have to start all over again. Before the war boatmen on the Tweed would not hear of fishing with anything but sprats. All the big catches in the thirties were made with them, and it needed another man doing nothing all day but sit on the bank mounting them if you were to land thirty fish in the day.

Find out what the fashion is on any river you fish, and if you have the strength of mind to ignore hotel bar advice, fish with something quite different. There are many different lures that are about equally attractive to salmon; but they are much more likely to take the first time they see any particular lure. If they have seen a succession of Toby spoons flashing through the pools all the way from Berwick to Kelso, your best chance will be with something quite different if you are fishing farther up stream. The only day I have fished on the Tay I caught a fish on a Toby because everyone else was fishing with a horrible looking thing called a Kynoch Killer.

A brown and gold minnow or a yellow belly are as good as anything. The yellow belly shows up well in coloured water. I use a brown and gold normally and sometimes a blue and silver on a bright day for a change.

I once had a wonderful day in March on about the best beat on the Tweed. I was fishing from the bank while my hostess was fishing from a boat. After lunch I heard her ask the boatman what I was fishing with, and his reply, 'I think it was once a brown and gold.' Rather shaming; but a bait that gets a bit dull and tarnished can be very effective. I hate losing baits when they have got broken in and are old friends. I caught 10 salmon on that one minnow that day, the only time I have ever done so.

When the water is a normal height and I am fishing from the bank I use no lead; just a metal minnow. It is so much easier to cast with only one weight, and there is no real point in fishing right on the bottom of the river. Anyway I can't afford to, it is so expensive in lost minnows. Salmon are used to feeding in the Arctic waters of the North Atlantic around Greenland. Here they chase and catch their food. Spring water in our rivers is no colder than the Humboldt current. They may appear glued to the bottom, but they can move fast enough if they want to, and will rise two feet from the bottom to take an attractive looking lure.

The usual way of fishing a bait is to throw it across and slightly down stream. It should land beyond the main current. You can wind in as it comes back across the stream or you need not do so, if your minnow isn't too heavy and the current is fairly strong. If you throw it more squarely across it will sink deeper, as it will if you hold your rod top low. You will soon learn to control the depth at which the minnow swims. If you fish without a lead and let it swim naturally through the currents and eddies, it can be most attractive to salmon, and it is worth varying the speed at which the minnow is fishing from time to time.

The first spring salmon is the most exciting of the year, as it is the best to eat; but one disadvantage of taking a beat early in the season is that the river may be too big and coloured to fish. That is what the boatman and other experienced fishermen will tell you, but is it really true? Just as you can catch fish on a fly when it appears hopeless, so you can with a minnow when it looks far far worse.

Most beats on salmon rivers have gillies attached, and on strange water a man with local knowledge is almost essential; but this has its disadvantages. On this particular morning it is still raining and blowing half a gale. The water drips off the gillie's mackintosh and long drooping moustache as he stands in the hall of your hotel holding a soaking cap in his red, weather-beaten hands. You have already looked at the swirling chocolate-coloured flood in the river before breakfast. He only has to say one word 'Hopeless' and you retire to your fire and daily paper without a murmur. Perhaps it is unfair to blame the gillie entirely, for every other local who knows anything about that river will tell you exactly the same thing.

Looking at a large river in spate it is almost impossible to imagine that you might catch a fish from it. The usual lies, which you fish when the gillie rows you, are a raging torrent, and quite big stones are being trundled down the river by the force of the current. The very lies themselves may be altering as you watch the river swirling past. The salmon quite obviously aren't out there; but, dash it all, if there are a lot of fish in the river they must be somewhere. One is apt to feel that with all that water coming down the fish must be more spread out than usual, but in fact exactly the opposite is the case.

They are indeed much nearer to you than they will be in three days' time, when the river has run in to a fishing height, for every single salmon in the whole river is within a few yards of the bank. They don't often show, but when you think about it, where else could they possibly be? The only place where there is an ease is near the bank. Here there are little eddies and backwaters behind lumps of earth and tree stumps left by previous floods. No salmon is going to face that torrent and risk being struck in the eye by a 2lb. stone when he can swim in comparative ease at the sides.

Even near the bank there are not many obvious places where you might expect a salmon to lie. In a mile of water there may only be forty yards in which you can detect possible lies when you go for a walk after lunch. And go for a walk you must, to recover from the sleepy feeling attendant on drinking three glasses of sherry before lunch, and your way is bound to take you to look at your expensive beat even if you can't fish it. Why not take a rod with you, it can do no harm? But first you mustn't mind what people think of you as an angler. If you want them to think of you as a knowledgeable fisherman you must hide the rod until you are out of sight; if you are seen with one everybody will think you are mad. You must also overcome the hopeless feeling that the general look and colour of the river will produce.

We are apt to judge the colour of water by the colour of our drinking or bath water and view any departure from it with distaste. Try comparing it with strong milky tea and you will feel much more optimistic. Don't forget that salmon are looking up through it at the light not down into it as we usually do unless we fall in.

When selecting a bait in these circumstances I don't think you can do better than a very large golden sprat, and fish with a heavy round lead attached to the ball-bearing swivel. It is not necessary to throw the bait more than 10 or 12 yards, as it wastes time fishing where there are no fish. Throw the bait square or slightly upstream and let it sink until you feel the lead bumping on the bottom. The fish will be right on the bottom where the current is slackest, so let your bait hit him right on the nose and he will have no excuse for not taking it. It is an advantage to know what the bottom of the river consists of. Where it is gravel you can let your lead bump along it; but where rocky you may get caught up. If you have fished the place at a normal height you will have seen it. But even if you do get caught up you will probably get the bait off again without much difficulty, as you will have such a short line out. It is when you get stuck on the bottom at the end of a long cast that you so often say goodbye to about fifteen shillings' worth of tackle.

When the river is very high and still rising after a drought you may have a bad colour combined with all kinds of debris floating down. Your swivels, lead and bait will be covered with the stuff after every cast. Then even I will admit that conditions are impossible with a spinning bait. As long as your bait remains clean, however big and dirty the water may be, I assure you there is a chance of catching a fish. The chance improves just as soon as the river starts to fall the least little bit.

In the early part of the season, on Tweed, the best catches are made in a big coloured water, fishing a sprat or some other large spinning bait. One day the boatmen all announce that 'she is too big and coloured', and the very next day practically every beat below Kelso has double figures. The critical height appears to be 4ft. at the gauge at Kelso bridge. Above that height no boat is launched, no bait is cast, and the anglers who fish these expensive beats accept this situation.

I don't blame the boatmen. They are indeed entirely right in saying that fishing from a boat in these conditions is hopeless. If you are too old or lazy to walk and fish from the bank then I fear you might as well stay at home. On these occasions it is an advantage to have a beat without a boatman. But if you have one, try to leave him at home. There is nothing more depressing than fishing to an audience who are convinced that you won't catch anything. They are usually so absolutely right.

Several years ago we had a very big flood in March. So big was it that our boat might have been in danger, as the river was over the bank where the post was driven to which the boat was tied. I went down to see, and as my rod was in the car—it usually is—I took it and rather shamefacedly put it up before walking down to the boat. There couldn't possibly be a chance as the river was over 7 ft. at Kelso, but one doesn't feel right walking along a river bank without a rod in one's hand. The boat was all right and just below it there was an ease over a gravel bottom opposite a steep 4ft. bank, the top of which the river was lapping.

The water had been an inch or two higher, and although the colour was as bad as it could be there was no debris coming down. I wandered along the bank throwing in my golden sprat, and allowing the ball of lead to bump along the gravel, hoping that nobody would see me and have me certified. Suddenly there was a great jerk and a fish went tearing out into the stream. It felt much too active to be a kelt but you can never be sure. I was most anxious to catch it as evidence that I really had hooked something; but it was not to be. A minute later the fish got off without showing itself.

It was most encouraging and I felt quite certain that the next morning would be a good chance. I rang up my brother and told him to get down as early as possible. He didn't believe a word of it because when I arrived at the river about mid-day he still wasn't there. The river was about 5½ft. at Kelso and still very coloured, but this wasn't worrying me. At the fourth cast I thought I had hooked a lump of bank at my feet, but in a second it began to move —the most exciting moment in fishing with a bait. The first fish of the day is always the most anxious one to play but I landed this all right, a lovely clean fish of 8lb., and I greeted my brother a few minutes later with a large grin. He could hardly believe it, and kept staring at the fish to convince himself it was real.

There were only two short places to fish, each about 20 yards long; but the fish were running so it didn't matter fishing them over and over again. We landed four clean fish and about the same number of kelts between us.

We had an audience for some of the time. The fisherman on the opposite beat came up to bail out his boat. He sat on the bank and watched. He couldn't very well say 'It's hopeless', as we held up a couple of fish for him to see on arrival, but each time he saw us hook and land another he shouted across, 'You'll never do it again,' 'It will only happen once in a lifetime'. I hadn't the heart to tell him that I had hooked one the day before. I also knew perfectly well that he was wrong. It would happen again given a high water and a stock of fish. It has happened again several times.

On a strange beat it is well worth trying in any likely looking place. It won't take long as there are not usually very many and they are quite small. There is an excellent chance of success on your very first try. If you are lucky enough to take the same beat for several years your previous knowledge will be of value, and you will come to regard a raging torrent with keen hope rather than despondency. Besides I think that for all of us there is a special satisfaction in catching a fish or two, when nobody else thinks it is worth trying.

I also know of places on two other beats on Tweed where one can catch fish when the river is over 5ft., but one isn't usually invited to fish under these conditions.

On one occasion finding the place was rather embarrassing. When we first came up here we lived in half the house belonging to a most charming elderly lady. We overlooked the Tweed, and the trout fishing at the bottom of the garden belonged to our landlady who let me fish. The salmon rights belonged to the estate opposite. One day an ex-P.O.W. friend came to stay to fish for salmon for the first time, on our beat on the Monday. On the Saturday I wanted him to practise throwing a minnow in preparation. There was a huge flood so we went down to the foot of the garden. You know the way it is, if you are casting a salmon bait you instinctively choose a spot where a salmon might possibly be. I started my demonstration in an ease over a fairly smooth rocky bottom which was usually dry and nowhere near any known salmon lie. At my third demonstration cast I hooked a salmon which we duly landed. Nobody had seen us; but what to do with it? I gave half to my friend and half to my landlady. Years later, when I knew him better, I told the owner of the salmon-fishing rights.

There is only one way of being really popular with all other salmon fishermen and that is by never catching a salmon. But if you do catch one, the method you employ will affect your popularity. There was one gentleman quite recently who took a famous and much sought after beat on the lower Tweed for the second half of February. He celebrated the opening of the bait season on the 15th of February by fishing with a prawn all day long and with nothing else. He caught ten fish and the memory of those fish will have to compensate for the fact that he will never be permitted to take that beat again. He would have caught just as many on a minnow.

Nobody should mind if you fish a large river in a big

water in the spring with a minnow, provided you are not breaking a river-board rule. Anyone has a right to be annoyed if you hurry down and fish a pool in the summer with a prawn before they have a chance to fish it with a fly. A prawn used out of place seems to stir most fishermen from their usual placid calm and arouse furious indignation.

When the river begins to warm up and the water becomes lower a small fly can often be the best method of fishing; but if it doesn't work there is a number of other ways of fishing which may prevent your day from being blank. These are prawn fishing and worm fishing, and I shall deal with them separately later. If you use a prawn you may make enemies; but fishing a worm is rather like not being able to pronounce the letter 'H'. It is likely to arouse only slightly amused and condescending contempt.

The success of any method depends very largely on the skill of application. Your specialist will always do best. On any large river there will always be experts at any particular method. The Tweed has its expert at fishing a plug, its worming expert, upstream minnow expert. There was a real artist with a prawn and what a charming and generous man he was, too. If you talk fishing to people you will soon discover who the experts are. The next step is to meet them, talk to them and if possible see them at work. Copy their methods at first, and later introduce variations of your own because you will often find that their technique is limited to fishing on one type of water. By making alterations you can often adapt it to other water conditions.

How much fun and interest the fly-only man misses if he did but know it!

Before you start fishing with a bait on any new river, make quite certain that you are breaking no local rule. These vary with every river and often from beat to beat on the same river or with the water height. Even if there are no rules it is a good idea to sound out the feelings of other fishermen, particularly on the beat opposite.

Remember that a gentleman never annoys anyone—unintentionally.

Possibly the first alternative to a fly is a small minnow fished down and across the stream. Early on you use a minnow of up to 3ins. With a low water you go down to 1½in. or 1¼in.

There is another way of fishing a small minnow which has many advantages: it doesn't seem to disturb a pool in the slightest and it requires considerable skill. It is also one of the most exciting ways of catching a salmon and is often very effective. For this last reason it may arouse the resentment of other anglers which I feel is unjustified. Perhaps the chief advantage of the method is that it works best in a bright sun and is complementary to the small fly; when fish won't take one they will often take the other.

I use a 1¼in. or 1½in. black and gold minnow, but the colour probably isn't important. You start at the bottom of the pool and wade out as far as you can to get directly below the bottom lies. The minnow is thrown directly upstream and reeled in as fast as you comfortably can with a multiplier or fixed spool reel. The minnow should be kept near the surface, certainly not deeper than 1-2ft. The next cast is at a slight angle across the stream and the final one right across the farthest lie. The number of casts depends on the size of the pool and the accuracy of your casting. You want to cover all the lies. Don't reel in so quickly when fishing across the stream, but keep your minnow high in the water by raising the rod point. You then wade 4 or 6 yards up the stream and start again. If however there is only one place that is holding fish you can stick to it for 20 minutes or so. Sooner or later a fish may well make a grab at the minnow.

They take in a variety of ways. Often they grab it as it touches the water and you think the minnow must have sunk quickly on to a stone before you started reeling. Sometimes they follow it right down to your feet. Quite often they take as they are swimming fast downstream and don't turn back to their lies for an appreciable time. These fish can be difficult to hook. If they do turn with it you feel a tremendous tug because you are reeling in so fast.

If you are fishing a large river like the Tweed you may think you are fishing quite accurately. It is only when fishing a very small river like the Dorset Frome that you realise how inaccurate you really are. When the fish are lying within a yard of the bank my minnow often lands among thistles or rushes. I must present an amusing spectacle crawling about trying to retrieve it without scaring the fish.

I went and fished on the Frome again fairly recently. My host graciously allowed me to try the upstream minnow, although he has come all over pure lately and never fishes for salmon with anything but a fly—preferably dry. I think his change of attitude was helped by the fact that he had hardly caught a salmon on his beat that year. Not for one moment did he expect me to have any success with a minnow and he had thoroughly disapproved of an article I had recently had published on the subject.

During the two days we fished Brenda caught a very exciting one on a fly while I caught and lost one on a minnow. Just before we were due to leave on the second day we all forgathered above the mill where most of the fish in the beat were concentrated.

'Go on,' said my host, Uncle A. 'Now just show us how it should be done,' a remark well calculated to put me off. We knew where two or three fish were lying, so I went and stood just above a very low bridge called 'The Bunny', and immediately below the fish. Brenda, my host and his nephew Anthony stood on the bridge, two of them preparing to make derogatory remarks when nothing happened. For once I was fairly accurate and did at least manage to land the minnow in the river at each cast. To everyone's astonishment, although I disguised mine, a fish of about 12lb. took at the fifth cast. All went well until he was nearly played out, when he was swept down through the bridge at the feet of the spectators. Sixty yards below were the hatches into the mill pool. Without a moment's hesitation Anthony threw off most of his clothes and waded out into the very strong current, at the considerable risk of being sucked through the hatches like a hair down the plug hole of a bath. I couldn't see what was happening because of the bridge, but I was not without advice from those standing on the bridge. Anthony found the fish hiding under a weed bed and managed to gaff him and get ashore again without falling further in or dropping the gaff; a remarkable performance. What it is to be young and enthusiastic.

The following weekend Uncle A continued to fish punctiliously with his fly and as usual nothing whatever happened. Finally, as he admitted later, he was tempted from the straight and greasy line and tried throwing a minnow upstream himself. He soon discovered that it is more difficult to be really accurate with a minnow than with a dry fly. Using polaroid glasses, which helped him to see into the water, he was trying to tempt a fish that looked all of 40lb. I think he was using a spoon but he wouldn't tell me. He could also see a smaller fish lying some distance from the monster. He was fishing away and glanced towards where the smaller one was lying. It wasn't there. He was just thinking 'That's funny' when it took the bait at his feet. Fancy catching the wrong salmon. Oh shame!

I don't think it is the bait that really matters so much as the method of presentation. Something whisking downstream past a fish can prove most effective. A minnow is easy to control and as good as anything, but it doesn't much matter what you fish with.

A few years ago my brother Mark was fishing on the Tweed and suffering from swan trouble. This is the real or imagined disturbance of a pool by a flock of about ten mute swans. One can't imagine that all those long necks, with those stupid heads on the end of them, can do much good guzzling about among the salmon lies. If no fish are taking it is easy to blame those stupid protected birds. On this occasion Mark was fishing a Toby spoon normally down stream. The flock of swans was disporting itself just upstream of him. Eventually his inability to catch a fish, coupled with the sight of the swans so obviously enjoying themselves, proved too much for his equanimity. With a horrible oath he flung his Toby spoon at the nearest swan. He missed and the swan moved away in some alarm. Determined to have another shot before it was out of range, he reeled in as fast as he could. A salmon took the spoon almost directly below where the swan had been a moment before. There was a terrific kerfuffle on the surface of the water and then it got off again.

An ordinary metal Devon fished in the way I have described does not alarm the salmon in the least; but the upstream minnow can be abused. If you use a very heavy or a lead minnow, or if you reel in too slowly, there is a strong possibility that you will start foulhooking salmon: especially if there are large numbers of fish on the lies. Salmon balance themselves in a current by extending their pectoral fins, and it is here that they are most likely to be hooked. We all occasionally foulhook fish and it is excusable; but you should not make a habit of it. Another reason why it is a mistake, apart from fishing ethics, is that the fish nearly always gets off, and it never forgets its experience. The next time it sees a minnow or even sometimes a fly, it dashes about the pool in alarm. This disturbs all the other fish in the pool as well, and they are unlikely to take.

One argument against using the upstream minnow as I have described it is that it catches too many salmon. But don't forget that you can catch double figures of salmon with a small fly and surface line. Perhaps to fish the upstream minnow requires more skill. I think that if it is considered that too many fish are being caught it would be wiser to limit the number of fish one rod may keep in one day, rather than the method of angling.

The thrill of catching a salmon on an upstream minnow is just as great as on a small fly. You so often see the fish in the water and actually see it open its mouth and take. As you are reeling in you see the minnow first, glittering in the clear water. Then a great shape looms up behind it; there is the fish, not 10 yards away; you see it take and turn away with the minnow in its mouth. Then comes the jerk and a rush as he goes tearing off upstream. Fish caught in this way are very often well hooked, sometimes right down the throat.

In the summer a natural minnow can be a very good bait. I catch them in a minnow trap and put them straight into a tin of salt, which kills them almost at once. You can mount them on a pin with a spinning flange or you can make them rotate slowly when pulled through the water by putting a bend in them. This is done with a plain pin or with two treble hooks, one attached at the head, the other near the tail. Fished in this way, above the lip of a cauld, they can be most effective. They look just like a small fish that is sick, and it is the natural reaction of wild animals and fish to kill anything that is abnormal or ailing.

If you don't catch a salmon you can always have 'whitebait' for supper. Take the remaining minnows out of the tin of salt that evening and run them under the cold tap; roll them in flour and cook them in deep fat until they are crisp and brown. They really are awfully good; but don't tell your guests where they come from. There is an instinctive aversion to eating salmon baits which is probably not unconnected with the smell of fishing bags from which they emerge.

I remember the alarm among our guests, several years ago now, when Uncle from the Frome and I were preparing supper for friends who owned the hotel on which we were based. Uncle was out of the room when they arrived and I explained that the salmon was going to have a very special prawn sauce, and A had gone to get the prawns out of his fishing bag.

'Oh, no,' they cried. The looks of consternation on their faces were all I could have wished for. I let them think about it for the few moments until A returned bearing a packet of prawns fresh from Billingsgate that very morning. But the contents of the packet still had to be examined and smelt before I was allowed to stir them into my white sauce.

A day's salmon fishing is far too short to allow one to try even one in a hundred of all the different lures available in their varying colours and sizes. If you are fishing with a friend it is rather fun for each to try different baits. In this way you can experiment with twice the number, and compare results.

The most rapidly increasing types of baits are the plugs and spoons. Each time you go into a tackle shop you are confronted with a new selection. I have seldom caught a salmon on a plug, but I am told by the experts that the secret of a good plug is that it should have plenty of wiggle and darting motion in slack water. Spoons come in all shapes, sizes and colours, all having a different action in the water. Besides the new models there is a mass of home-made ones, which can be bent to make them do practically anything in the water.

Salmon quite definitely have their preferences, but whether these vary from time to time and place to place I find it hard to decide. Different speeds of current may suit different designs of plugs and spoons. The large Toby spoon must be about the most popular at the moment. It can be deadly fished in a quick run without a lead. You throw it out and let it swim through the stream without reeling, like fishing a fly. Only after it has reached your side of the stream do you reel in. The smaller Toby is not nearly so effective because its action is quite different. It doesn't dart about and flash nearly as much as the big one does.

The Mepps spoon works on another principle and has

an entirely different action. There are several other types working on the same principle. A spoon revolves round a stationary shank, at the end of which the treble hook is fixed. The spoon continues to revolve even when it is moving slowly through still water. I have caught salmon on them, but I think they are more effective for sea-trout and brown trout in smaller sizes. Salmon seem to prefer something that changes direction and looks like a small fish trying to escape.

If you fish with spoons you will soon develop a prefer-ence for one kind, and I would never advise anyone to change from their favourite. You may well have hit on the most attractive way of presenting this particular spoon, and presentation is all important.

If you want a change I would advise trying one of a different shape rather than of a different colour. I think silver is as good a colour as any other and changing to another won't make much difference. The longer you fish the less often you change your bait.

I am no handy man—ask my wife—and anything I make other people could most certainly make, probably better and more quickly. But I find it is well worth making mounts for minnows as my minnows are expected to outlive several mounts. Besides, if you make your own you can use any size of treble hook you like with any size of minnow. All you need is a selection of eyed treble hooks, a reel of elasticum wire, a pair of pointed pliers, a selection of swivels which will fit your minnows, and a child's toy bead necklace. Individual beads are ridiculously expensive.

Cut off a length of elasticum wire, thread one end through the eye of the treble, round between the bends of the hooks and back through the eye from the opposite direction. Pull it taut and twist it up. Slip on the bead, measure the length of twisted wire required against your minnow and make a bend. Put on the swivel and complete the bend so that the doubled and twisted wire comes back on itself. Finally twist these two together for about an inch and cut off the free end.

It takes no time and saves about 2s. 6d. each time. It also enables you to discard any hooks that become blunted or lose their barbs. It often happens that one barb comes off. This quite definitely does matter. Don't say to yourself, 'Oh, well, two are still all right' and go on fishing with the defective hooks or you will lose a fish. Always keep the points of your treble hooks needlesharp as you should for use with a tube fly.

I get angry if my minnow catches on the bottom and I try not to fish deep enough for it to do so; but it is easy to misjudge the depth and current speed in a strange pool. There are various types of 'otters' which you can fit on the line to slide down and so disengage the hooks from the bottom; but they take up room in a fishing bag. I only carry a chicken ring, which I attach to an empty bottle, easily found on most river banks, with a length of nylon. This I twist on to my line and, while standing as far upstream and out in the current as possible, allow to float down the current. When it arrives above the hooks it will usually disengage them from a rock, but not from a tree stump or length of wire brought down by a flood. If eventually you must break, remember the spot, and when the river runs low see if you can recover your minnow. Quite often you will be able to re-stock your minnow tin with other contributions as well as your own. It is always worth while keeping your eyes open while walking along a river bank. It is surprising what you can pick up in the way of fishing tackle, and it gives you an idea of what other people are fishing with.

2. PRAWNS

It is fortunate for us fishermen that he who will be on the gate through which we all must pass was himself a fisherman of note. He will remember the irritations of his calling when other less skilful fishermen caught more than he. Let us hope he will make allowances for our occasional fits of temper and any uncharitable thoughts we may have while pursuing our favourite pastime. But I wonder how he will greet the man who was directly responsible for much of this discord; the man who first discovered that salmon take prawns in fresh water. I fear that this little whiskered crustacean has caused, and still does cause, much friction among salmon anglers. It is in the discoverer's favour that he passed on the information; or did his fellow anglers have to hide in the bushes to find out the secret of his phenomenal success?

Once when I was on the panel of a fishing 'Any Questions', I was asked why prawns create such discord among anglers. My answer was that salmon are less likely to ignore a prawn than any other bait. Sometimes they take it freely when they will take nothing else, but, more important, it quite often frightens them. A prawn can chase salmon off the lies and even out of a pool.

For the fly-fisherman it is irritating to see an angler on the opposite bank armed with prawns, removing fish after fish from a pool. It is even worse to see or imagine fish leaving a pool under their own steam for a beat further upstream.

If prawn fishing becomes too much of a habit it is a bad habit. One deterrent to its becoming a habit should be the fact that people who constantly fish with prawns sometimes get to look like one; the same colour, whiskers above the eyes, the lot.

You should always bear in mind that prawns may be socially unacceptable. If you own a whole river, you can do as you please; but most of us fish a beat, often with someone else fishing from the opposite bank. Never fish with a prawn as a guest or tenant without first asking permission, and if this appears to be given reluctantly don't use one if you want to be asked again. Since I began fishing with an upstream minnow I find that I use a prawn less frequently, but if there is no objection to fishing with one I still do so occasionally. There are times when there are plenty of fish about and all of them refuse to look at flies or minnows. Even if you scare a few, and make them go for a swim, it can't do much harm. After a while it becomes infuriating to be continually ignored by hundreds of enormous salmon. If you throw a prawn in among them there may be some response, and who knows but you may even catch one.

The very first fish I ever caught was on a prawn, long before I knew the controversy it might cause. Many years ago now, an uncle took a beat on the Wye and kindly asked me to fish. We all fished for a very long time and continually caught the bottom, but nothing more exciting. Then one day most unexpectedly, when I thought I had hooked it again, it began to move. This can be as exciting a moment in salmon fishing as any other, when something very heavy and very deep moves away upstream. You long for the first sight of it, and then you see a great bar of silver flash deep in the clear water.

The biggest fish I had previously caught was a sea-trout of 8lb. I thought the one I had hooked looked enormous, but I wasn't unduly excited as I thought perhaps all salmon looked as big as that. I just kept on pulling away at the piano wire trace until the fish became exhausted, and the gillie, Pittaway by name, gaffed it. It weighed 32lb. It took thirty-six years before I caught another fish of over 30lb.

If you decide to fish with a prawn and risk frightening the fish out of your pools you must be aware of the fact and on the look-out for danger signals. I never have the faintest idea how salmon will react to a prawn until I try one. It is no good looking at the sky or the river for inspiration, they won't tell you a thing. You must fish with a prawn for twenty minutes or so, in a pool where you know there are salmon and observe closely what happens. If you see fish jumping or showing off the lies, stop at once because it means the prawn is frightening them.

If they are going to take, something will probably happen pretty soon, so there is no point in continuing for very long if you don't have a touch. I don't believe in trying to bully a fish into taking a prawn. It may work sometimes but it is more likely to scare the fish in the end.

A delightful friend of my father's, Claud Pease, who lived in County Durham, used to tell of an experience on a Scottish river. One day he suggested trying a prawn and the gillie replied, 'It's no' a prawn watter.' But in spite of this he decided to give it a try. When he had landed the seventh salmon in an hour the gillie still shook his head and said, 'But it's no' a prawn watter.'

You can catch salmon on a prawn when the river is high or low, clear or coloured. At one time I thought that salmon didn't take prawns in a big coloured water. Then one day, when the river was big and still quite coloured after a flood, two friends went to fish our beat and I joined them for lunch. They were delighted with themselves when I arrived. John had been rowing while Alice fished, and they had caught two salmon and lost a third. I glanced at the prawn they had been using and couldn't help remarking, 'You know, most people put them on the other way round.' John looked at his, which had the spinner in the head and was attached to his nylon by it, and said, 'I didn't think it looked quite right myself.'

Up till then I had always been rather particular how I mounted my prawns; but if salmon don't mind whether they are travelling head first or tail first through the water, it can't matter very much how you mount them.

There are many ways of mounting prawns and every prawn fisherman has his own method of doing this. Some end up with a neat and tidy looking bait, others with one that looks as if it had lost an argument with a thorn bush. But don't worry; if salmon are really keen on taking a prawn they will even take one that has nearly come to bits and is only held together by yards of copper wire.

You can mount them on a single hook, on a plain

straight pin, or on a pin with a spinner. Then you can fish
them in various different ways, with or without a lead.
You can make them swim up and down with a sink-and-
draw motion, or let them swim through the current at an
even speed, fast or slow, depending on how you reel in.
You can tie them on with copper wire or pink elastic.
However you do it you will catch some fish but never all
of them.

I once heard that a prawn fished with a float was so deadly
that it had been banned on some rivers. If true this seemed
to be just what I had been searching for all my salmon
angling days. I hastened to collect some corks, and in one
of them I made a slit into which I slipped my nylon. Then
I flung the prawn, lead and cork out into the river and
waited in keen anticipation. Watching a float is a fascinating pastime, usually denied to salmon fishermen. I hadn't
long to wait until the cork was slowly pulled below the
surface where it stayed. After a while I reeled in the slack
until I was in touch and struck like mad. I hooked the
bottom. This continued to happen at frequent intervals
until I pushed the cork nearer the lead. Then nothing at
all happened for a very long time until quite suddenly the
cork started bobbing up and down and making unexpected
little rushes here and there. When I could bear it no longer
I tightened and a fish went tearing off up the river. It
played in a most peculiar way all over the place and sometimes nearly on the far bank. Eventually I discovered the
reason. It was a very large fish hooked in the extreme tip
of the tail. When I eventually landed it, after a good deal
of difficulty, I found that it was a kelt.

I always mount my prawns in the same way and try to
make them spin slowly but evenly. I use a pin with a spinning flange which I push up the straightened body of the
prawn from the tail to the head. For hooks I use two small,
very sharp trebles mounted well apart. One transfixes the
prawn's body and the other is right out behind it level
with the tips of its whiskers. I hold everything in place

with fine copper wire. I think the trailing hook stops one losing quite as many fish as one usually does when fishing with a prawn.

When a salmon takes a prawn it usually crunches it to break the shell. If it is holding the bait really tight, it is much more difficult to hook it firmly. The hook embedded in the prawn's body is not as likely to hook the salmon as the one out in its whiskers.

A fish will often crunch a prawn two or three times while swimming towards you so that you hardly feel it, before it turns away with it in its mouth. This accounts for the large number of prawns that are broken and mutilated without the fish being hooked. I think that this shows that in spite of being such an unnatural colour, salmon undoubtedly recognise what they are. They know that they have a hard shell which must be broken before they can be comfortably swallowed. They also take them better if they are made to swim with the motion of a startled prawn. This I discovered entirely by chance.

I find it quite easy to get overwinds with even the most foolproof of multiplying reels. I got one while throwing a prawn into a wind one day. While stripping off short lengths of line to untangle it I inadvertently imitated the short, rather quick jerks with which a prawn progresses backwards through the water when it is alarmed. Until then I had moved nothing, but when the prawn behaved in this way it was immediately seized by a salmon. Fortunately I had reached the bottom of my bird's nest just in time to play the fish. I caught three more in rapid succession by presenting the prawn in the same way.

Now when my prawn is coming over a lie in a quick stream, I often let it drop down a foot or so once or twice by letting the drum of a multiplying reel revolve freely and then stopping it with my thumb. It was fortunate that I realised that I had imitated a startled beastie. Those days at Bamburgh wading about in the rock pools trying to catch shrimps with the children, and observing their action when they escaped, were not wasted. But then, for an angler, observing anything in the sea or a river is never a waste of time.

Salmon don't seem to be much affected by the colour of prawns; pale ones or bright pink ones are taken equally readily. I also doubt whether salmon have much if any sense of smell. Eels hunt almost entirely by smell. If you are fishing a small clear Highland stream with a worm you can see eels hurrying up from pools downstream, attracted entirely by smell. Trout combine the senses of sight and smell when looking for food. They will often follow a metal minnow, but seldom take it. If you put on a freshly caught natural minnow they will take it at once; but it loses its attraction as soon as all the slime is washed off the skin. Once the skin begins to feel rough and no longer slimy you must mount another minnow.

I prefer fishing with fresh prawns from the point of handling them. The least expensive way of buying them is by the pound from a fishmonger. I put mine in a polythene bag with a handful of coarse salt, and pop them in the deep freeze.

But things don't always work out quite this way. After a warm spell in May your wife complains of the smell. In your fishing bag you discover a dreadful packet of rotting prawns. Then you find that you have run out of fresh ones so you have to fish with them. You can hardly bear to touch them and they fall to bits as you try to mount them; but the salmon don't seem to mind and take them nearly as readily as they take fresh ones. Eating your lunch isn't much fun though.

In shops you can buy prawns in bottles or in packets, preserved in formalin or glycerine. Salmon don't mind any of these tastes either.

You can now even get plastic ones. The most realistic ones are made in France and are provided with tubes of concentrated prawn smell which you squeeze into 'Une Orifice'. This will influence the angler if not the salmon.

3a   Camasunary river mouth

3b   Fishing the Sea Pool

4a   Dry-fly on the Fisherman's Pool

4b   Playing a fish in a spate, Camasunary river

The most popular sizes and colours of prawns, and methods of fishing them, vary from river to river. Many rivers have their own experts who catch more fish with a prawn than anyone else; other fishermen try to copy their methods and so a universal technique is developed. But don't be too disheartened if you go to fish a new river and are told that your well-tried methods are all wrong. At least give them a try before attempting to alter them.

One year I was very kindly lent a beat on the Irish Blackwater, complete with a house and a car. There was also a splendid character called George Bolster to show us where and how to fish. My two brothers and our wives made up the party. We were told to catch as many salmon as possible by all legitimate means, so I took a packet of freshly salted prawns as part of my offering.

George Bolster was an expert at fishing with everything and a real master with a worm for salmon and trout. When he caught the bottom while fishing for salmon with a worm he would wait patiently for an eel to come and unhook him. He knew when it was there, too, and used to give a running commentary on events nobody could see, and only he could feel, happening on the bottom of the river.

'He's there. He's at it now. He canna get it off, no he canna. There he's got it now,' as he lifted hook and eel safely ashore.

He didn't think anything of my prawns, which probably came from Scandinavia. He said the Blackwater salmon would only take the Galway Bay prawns, 'the little fat fellows.' His cousin was going to send him some straight from Galway and we wouldn't catch a fish on a prawn until they arrived. Nor did he think anything of my way of fishing a prawn, for he never made his spin.

So we fished with everything else for three days and caught three fish, two on worms and one on a fly. George also fished all the time but without success. There were very few fish in the water and we only knew of about half a dozen in the whole beat.

D

Then one morning, when on my own, I decided to try my prawns. I had three fish on the bank by the time the others arrived for lunch with one between them. Two were old friends and one was a fish we hadn't seen move.

The cousin's 'little fat fellows' never did arrive while we were there, so we had no chance of comparing them with our own.

I have since been told that Galway Bay prawns are in fact crayfish and not prawns at all. George Bolster was certainly right that salmon which had been feeding on them recently in the sea would prefer to take them in fresh water. But my prawns were not very different and, fished in my own well-tried way, were very effective. We caught several more fish on them in the next few days.

We didn't catch very many fish during our week's stay but this did not affect our enjoyment which was tremendous. The Irish are all sportsmen whether they ride horses or go fishing, and they are the best of company. Even a blank day is delightful when you are told stories of the countryside, and great fishermen catching large salmon from the pools you are fishing.

The countryside has a charm all of its own: the little green fields with brilliant yellow gorsy banks between them, stretching up to brown moors and the blue sky; the fresh clear air and the sparkling water.

Not many fresh fish seemed to be coming forward; but considering the numbers of fish about we did quite well, and by the time we left most of the familiar splashings were stilled for ever. George's parting remark was a great compliment. He said, 'It will need a professor to catch them now.'

Prawns, crayfish or shrimps of the right size will all catch salmon. In low water some people fish a shrimp on a single hook with a fly rod, and this can be deadly. The variations in technique are endless and you could fish for salmon the entire time using nothing but crustacea of various kinds, in different ways, and never exhaust all the

possibilities of attracting them. But you would not catch
nearly as many fish as the more versatile man who fishes
with fly and minnow, and occasionally with a prawn and
worm.

Unfortunately kelts are as keen on taking prawns as are
fresh salmon. I am far too parsimonious to enjoy feeding
prawns to the creatures at a shilling a time. It is bad
enough when they chew up the prawn and get off; but
worse still when you have to play and land them. Unhook-
ing a kelt with frozen fingers from a prawn tackle while it
kicks and struggles and bites you is agony. No disgorger will
work when there are two trebles way down a fish's throat.
Perhaps the best thing to use is a pair of long-nosed pliers.

Only occasionally, and in desperation for a clean fish,
do I try a prawn before the kelts are out of the water. The
first time salmon see a prawn can be very effective.

The actual catching of a fish on a prawn can be just as
exciting as on anything else. Usually the take is a deep
savage tug after perhaps the suspicion of a touch a moment
before. But sometimes you actually see the salmon come
and take.

A chalk stream is the place to see a trout take a fly, so
if you fish for salmon in one you should sometimes see the
take. Just after the war I was lucky enough to fish the
Dorset Frome fairly often, but for several years I never
actually saw a salmon follow my bait. Meanwhile A, who
was a keen prawn fisher in those days, kept seeing salmon
dashing about the river after his prawns. He used polaroid
glasses, which I told him was unfair unless you could fit
them to the salmon as well. He replied that even without
them I should often see a salmon turn at my bait in the
water if I wasn't blind. However, there it was, I never
did—until a certain week-end in May.

A had to return to London on Sunday night, while I
stayed on for another day's fishing. The weather was very
cold but bright, and he had discovered that by far the best

chance of hooking a salmon was between 7 a.m. and
10 a.m. so he left me with strict instructions to be out and
fishing by that unearthly hour.

When the alarm clock exploded at 6 a.m. the air about
my nose was distinctly chilly, but I left my bed and
looked out of the window. It might have been March, for
there was hoar frost on the grass of the water meadows,
and a white mist rising from the river one field away.

It seemed a most unlikely day on which to catch a fish
before breakfast; but I put temptation from me and
climbed into my very cold clothes. The hotel was still fast
asleep, but everything was ready in the kitchen. The top
of the Esse was red hot, with a kettle and saucepan handy.
The tea, eggs, milk, bread, butter and teapot were ready
on a tray. That's the sort of fishing hotel to stay in.

I felt warmer and more ready for the day when I had
dealt with that lot, and I mounted the hotel bicycle feeling
quite cheerful. It isn't far to the top of the fishing beat;
over the bridge and level crossing, and a quarter of a mile
on to the mill; but my hands were quite numb by the time
I got there. I had to flap them about before the fingers
were warm enough to mount a prawn, which was the bait
with which most people seemed to succeed.

I had left my spinning rod at the mill the night before,
but it was no use leaving a prawn mounted as a cat always
ate it. When everything was ready I set out to fish my way
downstream towards a fishing hut and a second breakfast
at a more reasonable hour.

The grass was soaking as the frost melted, but I wore
long rubber boots, which kept my legs warm and dry.
I started fishing at the mill pool, where only the day
before A had seen a salmon chasing his prawn, and
snapping at it like a terrier at a postman's trousers. But this
morning there might not have been a fish in the pool.

Below the mill pool the river winds its way through flat
rushy meadows. It runs silently, swirling deep under the
bushes on the outside of the bends and gliding more

rapidly over the shallower places. The white mist marked its course down the flat valley and made angling seem very unlikely to produce satisfactory results. I fished away in all the favourite places, flapping my hands from time to time to bring them alive again. One disadvantage of a multiplying reel is that a hand gets wet while braking the drum with the thumb. Most people now use monofilament spinning lines as they do not pick up nearly as much water as braided nylon.

Nothing had happened before I reached a pool called the Mayfly. Here, as I was reeling the prawn up the middle of the pool, the line drew tight, and then came a heavy tug. For a second I saw a great flash of silver in the depth of the pool; but then the line went slack and he was off; a pity. However, it was a great thrill which made me expect another pull at every cast. I began to fish far more carefully.

There is a pool a few hundred yards above the hut called 'The Last Hope'. It was reputed to be a good spot; but apart from one pull in a very high water I had never touched a fish there. The river runs round a sharp loop and the lie is on the outside of the bend, where the stream is deep and strong against a steep bank. The river was low with little current in the centre of the pool, and the bank on the outside of the bend, where I was standing, was nearly three feet above the water level.

Right in the middle of the bend, where the current strikes the bank, there is a low thorn bush about 4ft. high, which sticks out a little way over the river.

I began fishing several yards above the bush with a lovely red prawn. For once I had mounted it properly, and it spun beautifully even in the loggy water. I was throwing the prawn out into the shallow water beyond the current, and when it neared my bank I allowed it to sink deeper by lowering the rod point and reeling very slowly. The prawn moved with the stream as it came slowly up the deep water.

When standing two paces above the bush, as the prawn began working up the deep water, I felt a distinct knock, which I thought felt like a fish. I went on steadily reeling in, and nothing more happened until finally the prawn came into view on my side of the bush. I was just thinking how well it showed up in the water, when the most enormous salmon sailed up behind it, opened his great white mouth and seized the prawn in his huge jaws.

I was either paralysed or had great self-control, for I went on steadily reeling and I remember thinking, don't strike now, wait until he turns away with it and then give him such a jerk. In fact I never felt him at all. The line went slack when he took, because he was travelling in the same direction and faster than the bait. He carried the prawn about two yards upstream like a retriever dog, until he was about 6ft. away and almost directly below me. Then quite deliberately he spat it out, with considerable force. He opened and shut his mouth twice to make sure the prawn really had gone before he turned round and disappeared back into the pool again.

Seeing a huge fish of about 30lb. so very close was altogether too much for me. I was like a cocktail shaker in the hands of an expert, and I had to sit down on the bank to recover. Sometimes if one rises a fish on a fly or touches one on a bait, one has the feeling that it will probably come again. For some reason I knew that here was an angling certainty. This fish would take the prawn the very next time he saw it, if he was given a few minutes' rest, and the prawn was presented to him in exactly the same manner.

I gave him and myself five minutes to settle down. For once I managed to put the prawn just where I wanted it to go. Even knowing that he was going to take I was unprepared for the savagery of his attack, and my heart gave its usual bound as the rod was practically snatched out of my hands. There were silver flashes deep in the water as he wrenched his head from side to side trying to rid himself of the pull on his jaws. Then he came to the surface and

thrashed about, shattering the smooth calm of the pool
and throwing spray in all directions. This is always an
anxious moment as it so often tears out the hold of the
hook; but this time the hook held and I saw that the prawn
was well back in his mouth.

When this didn't free him he began to rush about the
pool. First he went right up the middle through a patch
of weeds and for one awful moment the line went solid
and dead, but it came clear before he turned back down
the pool again. He jumped twice, shaking his head and
falling back with a loud splash which sent waves across the
smooth surface of the water. For a while he played up and
down in the middle of the pool, and by keeping a steady
strain on him from downstream I began to tire him.
Gradually he came closer until he was burrowing under
the bank at my feet. He kept his head down but every now
and then his tail came nearly to the surface and within
reach of the gaff, but the bank was so high that I could
only have gaffed him a few inches above the tail, and I
didn't like to take that risk. Then he must have seen me,
for he sailed away into the deep water again, well out of
reach.

He was getting very tired and a minute later came to the
surface near the tail of the pool, where he wallowed slowly
from side to side. When he was just coming to the gaff,
quite exhausted, and I was kneeling down, he did another
roll over very, very slowly and the bait flew out of his
mouth.

For a second it seemed too awful to be true; but it was
and the fish sank slowly to the bottom of the pool. I could
see him quite clearly as he lay behind a small patch of
weeds in about 3ft. of water and 3 yards from the bank.
The bottom of the pool shelved from the far side, and
under my bank the water was about 4ft. deep.

There wasn't a moment to be lost, nor time to consider
ethics, because fish recover much too quickly. I tore all my
clothes off except for my shirt and pullover, and put my

thigh boots and hat back on again. I laid my rod down on the bank pointing directly at the fish, and, armed with the gaff, ran twenty yards downstream to where the river looked shallow. I waded out into the river; half way across it became rather deep, a try upstream seemed as bad, so I said 'To Hell with it' and waded straight ahead right into a hole only 4 yards across but 8ft. deep, and very cold it was. I swam out, gasping for breath, but still holding the gaff and wearing my hat. The water squelched in my boots as I stumbled out on to the far bank; but there was no time to empty them. I ran up to opposite my rod point, and waded carefully out into the river peering into the water ahead of me. The light from that side was hopeless and I couldn't see the bottom of the river at all, so I felt gently ahead of my feet with the gaff when I thought I was getting near the fish.

The first indication that I had reached him was when I kicked him in the ribs and he shot off upstream into the pool again, having completely recovered from his exertions. So that was that. I went straight ahead, up to my armpits in the water, and climbed out on to the bank from where I had started. When the excitement was over I realised that I was extremely wet and very, very cold. Luckily I had a few dry clothes to put on and somewhat strangely clad I hurried off to the hut for my second breakfast, which came out of a bottle from Scotland. As I drank my meal I wondered just how big that fish really had been. He looked very nearly 30lb. but I think in fact he would have been just under. Anyway he was a great old fish and I hoped to have the opportunity to do further battle with some of his children one day. After breakfast I went and gazed at the scene of disaster and wondered if there had been anything more I could have done to land that fish. It seemed impossible that such a small, calm pool could hold so large a salmon. One thing seemed quite certain. There couldn't be another fish in the pool, even if there was it wouldn't take, but there was

no harm in having a cast since I had my rod with me.
I cast my prawn from the same old place, two yards above
the bush. At exactly the same spot bang and I was into
another fish. For a wild moment I thought it might be
the same one, but it came to the surface a minute later and
I saw that it was much smaller. I also saw that it was
hooked right in the tip of the jaw. Almost at once it came
right over to my side of the river under the bank and swam
slowly upstream. He was fairly deep but within reach, so
I held the line tight to the rod with my left hand, flung
myself on to my tummy and gaffed him. Spray flew but
I had him ashore as the prawn fell from his mouth. He
weighed 19lb. Quite an exciting morning.

One seems to lose a higher percentage of salmon hooked
on a prawn than on a minnow or other bait which has only
one treble hook. You often land a number of fish without
losing one and then the next five or six get off. Luck is all
important, but there are things you can do to help it along.

I rather like to pull a fish right to the surface, and then
ease the pressure so that it doesn't thresh about on it. By
so doing you see what size of fish you have hooked, and either
tear out a very light hold, which would have given later,
or pull the hook really home into a horny part of the
mouth.

A large number of salmon are lost when they are practically within one's grasp, and these are much the most
agonising to lose. It is essential to choose as advantageous
a spot as possible for the final stages of landing a salmon.
If you use a gaff or tailer, or have a companion with a
landing net, you want to bring the fish within reach when
it is in about 3ft. of water, so you need to have fairly deep
water close to the bank or you must wade out some way.
But never get the fish between you and the bank, for it
will probably give one more rush, the line will touch your
waders and you will be broken. If you keep quite still and
make no sudden movement a salmon will often come
within reach in deep water and an experienced netsman

D*

will land him before he is completely played. Net, gaff, tailer or bare hands, whatever you use you need practice and you will make mistakes which may lose you a fish.

I have seldom used a tailer, but I had no alternative on the Eden a few years ago when my ankle was in plaster from a fall off a horse. I wasn't very mobile on the bank so my host kindly provided a boat, anchor, long rope and tailer. When I had floated about 60 yards down from the anchor a salmon took my fly. Luckily it wasn't very big as there was a strong current. When it was played I had great difficulty in getting it up within reach and putting the wire loop round its tail; I missed twice and had to reset the beastly thing while still holding on to the rod and playing the fish. I did eventually manage to get it out and avoid falling headfirst into the river—a sore disappointment to my host who was poised ready with a camera to record what he thought would be the inevitable outcome.

Before you can beach a salmon it must be completely played out. It may well come right into the shallow water two or three times, but it will still find a reserve of energy and fight its way back into the current. So make sure that there are no snags in the shallow water for the line to catch on. If you are going to beach a salmon you must choose a good spot, with fairly small smooth stones. It is well worth leading a fish quite a long way to find a suitable place. If you don't bother you are more than likely to regret it.

Quick action can sometimes save the day if you have a salmon half beached on to gently sloping shingle and the hook comes away. A companion can usually prevent it from escaping. You sometimes can by yourself if you run and use your feet, but not always. Quite recently I lost a fish at the very last moment, and managed to get between it and the river. I kept my feet together and tried to scoop him up on to the shingle with my hands, but he evaded me with ease. It was particularly infuriating because my wife had caught three, and it was the only touch I had that day. I received absolutely no sympathy from Edward, our host.

There is a great temptation to pull just a little bit harder during those agonising last few moments of playing a salmon. This you must not give way to, in fact it is a good plan to set the check of the reel a little bit lighter than you had it when you began playing the fish, and whatever you do, never catch hold of the line in your hand and try to pull the fish on to the beach. The direct pull will very often break a light hold on a fish's mouth.

There are a great many ways of losing a salmon and one is never too old to discover new acts of stupidity which will ensure that a fish will either break one or get off.

Tailing a fish by hand is quite easy if it is played out, but you can hardly hold on to an active fish that begins kicking. The larger the fish the more difficult it is to pick up by the tail with one hand. The bigger your hand the heavier the fish you can pick up—my limit is about 15lb. and any salmon larger than that I must play until I can slither him up the shingle by holding his tail and pushing. In deep water I have to get my fingers into his gills and drag him up on to the bank.

Most salmon are almost impossible to hook, and when hooked do everything they can to get off; but there were two salmon that seemed determined to give themselves up.

One evening in early summer, Bob Aitken from Jedburgh brought me two salmon he had caught on our beat on the Tweed. He is one of the most skilful and dedicated of anglers in the Borders, a beautiful fly fisherman and an expert with a worm. My brother Mark, who had been fishing in the morning, rang up at lunch time and said he had caught one and lost one on a prawn; then he had to go and do some work on his farm. Bob had been fishing in the afternoon.

He had caught both the fish he brought to me on a worm. One was hooked right down in the stomach and he had left the hook there as it meant cutting the fish open to retrieve it. This we next did in my kitchen. In fresh water a salmon's stomach is small and rather hard. This one was slightly enlarged. We recovered the worm hook; but about two inches beyond it, right at the tail end of the stomach, there was a hard lump. We opened it up and found that it was caused by half a prawn. The fish had taken in exactly the same place where Mark lost his in the morning. We know that salmon can't feed in fresh water; but this one gave two very good imitations of doing so on that day.

But there was one even more luckless salmon. Mark was having a dinner party one evening, for which he had promised to produce a salmon; always a rash thing to do. They weren't at all keen to take anything, but he eventually hooked one on a prawn in a pool which at one point has flat rock sloping into a deep backwater. He played the fish with great care, fully aware that he would probably hook no other. Only when it was quite exhausted did he very slowly pull it on towards the gently sloping rock to beach it.

The salmon was about 5 yards out and in 3ft. of water, coming directly towards the shore, when the prawn flew from its mouth and lodged in a thorn bush behind Mark. The fish was so tired that it just lay quite still in the water. Mark had no gaff or tailer so there was absolutely no way of getting hold of it. With his prawn firmly embedded in the bush, even the faint hope of foul hooking it did not exist.

The enormity and unfairness of the whole thing suddenly struck him and he rushed into the water in a fit of temper. The salmon was roused from its torpor and galvanised into action by this unexpected intrusion. It shot off as hard as it could go in the direction in which it was pointing; straight on to the shelving rock. Mark rushed after it, flung himself on top of it and seized it to him with his hands. When he told me about it afterwards he didn't know whether to be ashamed of his temper or delighted with his capture.

3. WORMS

Trout, sea-trout and salmon will all take worms in fresh water; but why do salmon do so? Do they remember the days when they were parr, two or three years previously, or do they associate them with something they ate in the sea? A bunch of worms, which most people use, must closely resemble a small squid. I am told that squid are more plentiful in Arctic waters than elsewhere. Worms fished in Iceland are particularly deadly, and in many if not all rivers their use is banned. Icelandic salmon would be far more likely to meet and eat squid in the sea than worms in the rivers in any quantities when they were parr.

Whatever they think a worm is, salmon take them in a way which is quite different from the way they take anything else the angler has to offer them. They usually just suck at a worm, perhaps marking it with their teeth, picking it up and letting it go again as it floats down a stream; they don't stop the free progress of the worm and will often follow it for 10 or 12 yards, just nipping away at it. Eventually they may swallow it or become bored with it and leave it alone.

When trout and sea-trout, which don't venture so far in the sea, take a worm they behave in a different way. Perhaps from this we can argue that salmon think they are eating a squid. Salmon will also take a bunch of worms spinning slowly against the current, which must look like a squid, but they will also take a single worm, as I have discovered when I have run short. It doesn't, however, really matter what they think as along as they take occasionally when you fish for them.

In the Summer, when the river has run in very low and salmon won't look at fly or spinner, many people fish with a prawn. The worm is an alternative bait which you can

use under these conditions. It was the original and
classical 'bait', used even before the natural minnow—
which was fished about 150 years ago on the Tweed.

The worm is still the only bait allowed on some rivers
in the summer. This was so on the River Awe, but I believe
its use has been prohibited now. When I fished there
I gathered from the evidence that it did more execution
among the eels than the salmon, certainly the bank was
littered with little dead eels. Even then you weren't
supposed to advertise the fact that you stooped to fishing
with a worm. When I walked into the cocktail bar of the
Loch Awe Hotel with my coat lapel festooned with naked
hooks the other anglers nearly swooned on the tartan
carpet.

For some reason it is considered terribly non-U to fish
for salmon with a worm, and you must never talk about it
in polite society. I don't suppose that 10 per cent of
modern salmon fishers have ever tried fishing with a worm,
let alone caught a salmon on one. If you want to find out
how to do it, or discuss the chances of catching a salmon
with one, you must talk to a member of the local angling
Association, or consult a keen and knowledgeable boatman.
It would be no use approaching a man who has taken an
expensive beat on the Tweed, and parked his Bentley by
the river side. If you mentioned the word 'worm' he would
not consider you a fit person to invite out to dinner to
meet his beautiful daughter. But there are exceptions. On
one occasion a distinguished major-general and a lady
M.F.H. called in at our house on their way north to fish the
Dee, where worm fishing was permitted. They were much
concerned with the temperature of the car boot, for it
contained a very large tin full of worms which had to last
their whole fishing holiday.

Why is there a prejudice against fishing with a worm?
Is it that people don't like getting their fingers dirty, or
could there be a connection with the Book of Genesis.
Worms are rather the same shape as serpents. Men who

spend hours wrapping prawns on to mounts seem reluctant to impale wriggling worms on to hooks. If you have a boat-man or attendant get him to do it for you, and if not don't be so squeamish, because a worm compares very favourably with a prawn as a bait for salmon.

One great advantage is that it will never disturb a pool or frighten salmon. For this reason it can have no adverse effect on a salmon taking a fly, or some other lure, on the same or subsequent days.

The first time a salmon sees a worm is by far the best chance of catching him. After that he shows less and less interest until he shows none at all, and will finally let the worm trundle past him hour after hour without moving a fin. So you need not persist with a worm for very long unless you have nothing better to do.

A worm has many other advantages. You are most unlikely to lose a fish you hook on a worm. If he takes it properly and you leave him alone, you will probably hook him right down in the stomach, and if not you won't hook him at all.

You can also fish with a worm when the bottom of the river is too impossibly foul and the water too full of detached green slime to fish with anything else. This is a condition that unfortunately frequently prevails in the Tweed after the middle of May. Green slime grows on the bottom and becomes detached when the sun gets hot and the temperature of the water rises. It is nothing to do with fertilisers being washed into the water, as you find exactly the same green slime in the rivers of Skye, where fertilisers have never been applied in living memory.

Anything moving against the current becomes covered with the beastly stuff at once, but as long as the worm floats down freely it remains clean and fish will take it. After each recovery you have to remove pounds of the muck from your lead and worm, which is a bit tedious, but you can at least fish when nobody else can.

Since I started fishing for salmon with a worm, I have

learnt, by observation and questioning, all I can of the methods of everyone I meet who uses them. Each expert has devised his own technique, which is slightly different from anyone else's. They are all successful in the types of water in which they fish; but you often find that they catch all their fish in one or two similar places. You must modify your methods slightly to suit the type of water you are fishing.

You can use a fly or a spinning rod, a fly reel, a multiplier or a fixed drum reel, and any combination of them. So, unlike most forms of angling, no special equipment is required and you can try a worm with anything you happen to be fishing with.

I prefer a 10-12ft. fly rod with a multiplying reel. Most people put a small round lead or a few split shot on the nylon a foot or two from the worm. The hooks used vary considerably. Some use trebles, others 2 or 3 small hooks on a Stewart tackle, and yet others prefer single hooks of various sizes.

I prefer a single, fairly large hook. It is easier to put several worms on if the hook is without an eye and whipped on to the nylon. You can then push the first one right up the nylon out of the way.

When whipping a hook to nylon there are two things to remember. You must whip in sufficient to allow you to bend the end back over the whipped portion and tie that in as well. Nylon is so stretchy that unless you do so it invariably pulls out, even if you flatten the end you are whipping with a pair of pliers and use the stickiest varnish you know. But whatever you do avoid whipping the actual bend in the nylon. If you make nylon kink really sharply it is worse than tying a knot. It will break without warning with only the gentlest pull.

The worms used are usually the large brown ones. You can dig them up in wet weather in any well-manured ground. My wife complains that the only time I do any digging in the garden is when looking for worms to go fishing. When the ground becomes very dry they are bad to find; but there is a fascinating alternative method of catching them. Go out on the lawn on a still clear night when the dew begins to form about 1 a.m. with a torch and a tin. All the biggest and fattest worms will be lying at full stretch with just the tips of their tails in their holes. Apparently they are intent on breeding, and if you walk quietly you can catch hold of them. When you do they try to escape down their holes again, and if you pull too hard they come in half; but if you are patient they give up and can be extracted without being torn in two.

If you happen to be in the Western Highlands the search for worms is much more difficult, and a telescope may be of assistance. The first stage is to spot a horse or preferably a cow. Under the droppings you will probably find worms, but they will be miserable, half starved specimens compared to the ones you left at home under your well-kept lawn.

These large worms are pretty tough even when first caught, and they can be stored in moss for at least 10 days. Like most things they get tougher with age.

It is usual to fish with two or three worms, pushing the first ones up the nylon until you have covered the hook with the last one. You then pull them back down again so that they form a compact wriggling mass.

You only need about 2ft. of nylon between a small round lead and the worm. I attach my lead to a swivel, using a straightened paper-clip as a split-pin, so that the lead can become detached without breaking the nylon if it becomes caught in the bottom of the river.

The best water for fishing a worm is a fairly fast flowing stream. It is more difficult to fish a worm well in very fast or slow water. I like to wade out to within about 10 yards of the top lie and throw the worm 15 yards up and across the stream. As it floats down towards me I reel in and raise the rod point so that I can feel the lead bumping along the bottom all the time. If the line stops and the strain goes dead it means that the worm or lead has become caught in the bottom, never that a salmon has taken the worm, or is taking it; so try to dislodge it immediately, and keep it moving. If you leave it there hopefully, an eel will come and take it. When an eel gets hooked it takes no time at all to get under a stone, and then you really can say goodbye to your hook.

When the worm and lead have gone bumping down past me, I let the drum of the reel revolve freely so that the line follows freely downstream. I still keep in touch with the bumping lead, until it is 10 to 15 yards below me. Then I stop the line and let the worm swim through to my side of the current, and recover it slowly. If the lie is fairly wide you may need several casts from the one spot to cover it all. Then you can move 5 yards downstream before trying again.

When a salmon shows an interest in your worm it usually feels as though the lead is still bumping along the bottom, but occasionally giving a harder bump than you expect. You are now faced with the problem of what to do next. Some people strike fairly soon; but I have never had the least success by doing so with salmon—sea-trout are different. I leave my line slack and continue fishing in the same way, letting line go readily if the fish gives an extra hard bump.

The fish will often follow the worm all the way down, through the current and up your side of the stream as you reel in slowly. One of the first fish I caught on a worm did just that. Eventually I stopped reeling in and let the worm hang in the edge of the stream about 7 yards directly below me. I felt that the next move was his. For quite a while nothing happened. He had been so gentle up to then that I was quite unprepared for the savage wrench which eventually came. My fingers slipped from the handle of my multiplying reel and I got the most horrible overwind, as the check was off. Luckily there was plenty of slack line and I was able to undo the bird's nest and get the line straight on the reel while remaining out of touch with the fish. Eventually I tightened up to find out what went on at the other end. The salmon was still there, no doubt wondering what to do with the recent meal which he had swallowed, and we know he could not digest, for he had swallowed the worm and hook right down into his stomach. He was very well hooked indeed, and was duly landed.

If you strike and miss a salmon he will be frightened and not come again; but if you leave the worm free he may decide to swallow it after knocking it once or twice. You then feel a continuous gentle vibration. If this happens and you give him long enough time, you are almost certain to hook him right down in the stomach.

But there are days when salmon will mouth a worm two or three times the first occasion it passes them, once the second time, and thereafter ignore it entirely. I haven't yet discovered what you can do to hook them when they are behaving like that. On one occasion I went home and tied a special tackle: one hook for the worm and an extremely sharp small treble attached about 3ins. behind it with a piece of nylon, for the salmon. When the next two or three salmon came and sucked at my worm I struck hard and at once. Absolutely nothing happened except that I frightened the life out of the fish, which refused to take any further part in the sport.

There is another rather fascinating way of fishing a worm. You use a float and no lead and it is suitable for small rivers with low clear water. The distance between the float and worm should be roughly twice the depth of the water to be fished. You must fish a pool where there is an appreciable current, with fairly light monofilament line. The hook must be needle sharp, and the point must be exposed. You throw the float and worm out into the centre of the current and let them float unimpeded down the stream. The surface water flows more rapidly than the water at the bottom of the pool so that the worm is kept clear of the rocks by the pull of the float. You know when a fish is interested as the float begins bobbing and is then drawn under the surface. You cannot strike as the fish is too far away, and it must hook itself by pulling against the float, or at least be unable to spit out the worm until you can tighten and hook it. That is why you must use a fine and very sharp hook. The distance you let the float go is only limited by the amount of nylon on your reel and your eyesight. This might be a splendid way of fishing when standing on the bottom boundary.

One benefit of knowing how to fish salmon with a worm is that it enables one to fish places which hold salmon, and can be fished by no other method. There are many small salmon rivers which for part of their course run between high rocky cliffs, with rapid glides and deep swirling pools where no fly or minnow can be cast or fished properly.

The tributaries of the Tweed are like this in some places. The river is less than 10 yards wide, but each deep exciting pool may hold half a dozen salmon. After a flood in May a visit is well worth while. I had one delightful day beyond Selkirk with Hugh. Conditions were perfect; the water pale amber after a flood and the stones below it golden in the sunshine. The blossom was on the May trees and the cry of curlews and song of larks filled the air. Hugh knew every pool and every lie. The second one we fished was divided in two by the pillar of the arch of an old broken, ivy-covered pack bridge. I fished above it while Hugh tried the narrow rushing water below. Quite soon he hooked a salmon of 12lb. which went wild and tore up and down the rocky pool, jumping frequently. It is much more difficult and exciting playing a fish in a place like that than in a large pool. One jump landed him nearly on the far bank and a second later the strain went dead as the line got round an invisible rock. I just managed to wade across the river below the pool, on very slippery stones with the water within an inch of the top of my thigh boots. But I then found that I couldn't reach his line to clear it. Distances are deceptive when viewed from the other bank.

However, all was well, for the salmon eventually freed itself and was duly netted and admired.

In the afternoon we visited a most exciting pool; a deep rush and swirl below a high rock, where there were always several salmon. We scrambled down to the foot of the cliff just above the deepest part of the pool, and cast the worm up into the quick water, letting it sink and float down beneath us. I caught one almost immediately and then left it to Hugh while I went and explored the quick rocky run above. There was one deep little hole with white water at its head which cleared just before it broke again. From time to time I thought I could see a salmon's tail, then as it dropped a little further back, I was sure. It was only a yard or two away, so I knelt down and popped the worm in just above it. Sure enough I felt the familiar thrilling little tugs of a salmon at a worm, then I tightened and he was there. When I pulled him hard to begin playing him he was bound to run back down to the main pool. I was just planning my path over rocks and under trees when he got off. It was a pity as it was about to become most exciting. But almost immediately came a shout from Hugh and I ran back to help him. All went well until his salmon was nearly played when, with a series of rolls, it got the nylon wrapped round its body and went wallowing down on the surface to where the current quickened to leave the pool. There was no way to follow, with water 10ft. deep below, and a sheer cliff above, so Hugh held on and was broken. Thirty years ago we would have swum. But what a lovely day: two salmon on the bank, two lost and many more excitements. Each encounter gave the maximum thrill and shared pleasure.

Had we only caught one we should undoubtedly have shared it, but as it was we had one each to take home to our wives.

Worms play an important part in the diet of brown trout and sea-trout, and in the Borders a great many trout

are caught on them. Practically every small boy starts
fishing with them. After a flood you can see them hurrying
through Jedburgh carrying a variety of tackle, often
including a home-made rod with staples for rings. There
are also a few very old men I never see at any other time,
but who appear on these occasions carrying long whippy
greenheart rods with brass reels. They don't hurry from
pool to pool as do the young, but select a backwater at the
side of the stream, not too far from home, where they fish
away happily.

If you want to catch trout for a particular occasion and
the water is big and filthy dirty, fishing with a worm may
be the only method of doing so. If small boys with home-
made rods can catch fish, no advice on how to do so can be
needed from anyone. But if possible I delay my fishing
until the water has begun to clear, when you can usually
catch all the trout you need on a wet fly. If they won't
take a fly try a small Mepps spoon, but with it you are
apt to prick a lot of fish and fail to hook them.

Clear water worming is quite another matter and
requires delicacy of touch and accuracy in casting,
especially if you are fishing a small burn. In the early
morning the biggest fish can be caught in very thin water
in either rivers or streams. A fairly long rod is an asset,
and most people use small pink worms on a Stewart tackle,
very often with no lead.

One of the pleasures of fishing is recapturing the thrills
which one experienced when young. For many years
I neglected fishing for sea-trout with a worm, although
I was brought up on it. Somehow one thought it wasn't
quite the right thing to do; people might disapprove. One
advantage of getting older is that one no longer cares so
much what people think as long as one doesn't ever hurt
their feelings.

Even before my own children were old enough to be the
excuse, I started worm fishing for sea-trout again, and
what fun it is. On rivers it is completely complementary

to fishing with a fly. It about doubles the chances of catching fish, for when they won't take one they will often take the other. You use the same rod and nylon cast. All you need extra are some split shot, bare hooks and worms. You can change from fishing with one to the other in no time at all.

Whatever the height of the river I like to fish a pool with a fly first and then perhaps try a worm which can also be most effective in a low water. You must stalk the pool more carefully than you do when using a dry fly, because casting a worm is more difficult and you have to get that much nearer to the fish. It isn't at all easy to cast a worm far enough without dislodging it from the hook, which you certainly can't afford to do if they are Highland worms and you only have about six in the tin.

Sea-trout are very easily frightened if the water is low and there is no turbulence to hide you. You must crawl up and often lie flat on the bank when you reach the edge of the pool. You can fish without a lead or perhaps use a small shot, which helps in casting; throw the worm as far up and across the river as you can with a gentle swing of the rod, shooting the maximum amount of line which you have stripped from the reel and coiled down beside you. An Air Cel line is an advantage as it shoots so easily and prevents the worm from sinking too rapidly.

One day I found a big shoal of sea-trout in a pool in the Sligachan river in Skye. The water was low and as clear as anywhere in the world. Another pool is about 20ft. deep, and you can see the details of every rock on the bottom. I had to lie flat and roll down the bank to get into a little hollow within reach, but out of sight of the fish. I threw the worm out into the pool and a 2lb. sea-trout took almost as it touched the water. It tore about the pool scaring every other fish in it, but I managed to land it. I rested the pool for a few minutes before getting into position and trying again. The next time the worm was allowed to sink deeper before a fish of 1½lb took it.

They nearly always seem to take in order of seniority, finishing up with the smallest finnocks and finally tiddlers. On this occasion I ended up with six fish before they became disillusioned.

A sea-trout may take a worm hard and solid; but in a low water the line usually moves away in a series of short jerks. You should leave it until the line is dragging and you know that the worm is no longer moving downstream with the current. Then take up the slack and when you are in touch, strike sharply. It is fatal to give the line a little jerk when you first see it move, for this will always frighten that particular fish, and he will take no further interest. Some days fish swallow the worm. On others they only play with it, picking it up and dropping it again, and by striking sharply you will hook quite a number of them.

But in a spate is the real time to fish for sea-trout with a worm. Again I always like to try a pool with a fly first, because sea-trout will often take a fly better than they will a worm, especially if the river is starting to fall. When they have stopped taking flies you can usually catch one or two more on a worm.

There are always many places in a spate where you can't fish with a fly, but can catch fish with a worm. Pay particular attention to the rough water between pools. Sea-trout will probably be running and they rest in any little ease, behind a rock or under a bank. Wherever they rest they will take a worm.

A waterfall can be the greatest fun, because fish will always congregate at the foot of one; but fish your way up to it, popping your worm into every little ease you can detect.

It is probably still raining from a grey sky, with low scudding mist obscuring the mountain tops. You are constantly stepping over small burns, clear but bank high, hurrying to join the main river. Always try the spot where they run in, dropping the worm into the burn and letting it be swept out into the main river. A fish will take at once if he is there, so it only takes a second to fish each place.

The water pours from your macintosh and sou'wester; your hands are always soaking, but the wind is from the south and you are not cold. As you approach the waterfall the murmur of running water, which fills the air, becomes a roar; water crashes down over smooth black rock into a welter of boulders, an ever-changing scene of spray and falling water.

The waterfall on the Camasunary river in Skye is the one I know best, and I always find my feet hurrying as I approach it in a spate, and the excitement takes hold of me.

The biggest fall is at the bottom of a series of falls. Fish can only run up it when the river reaches a certain height, before that they congregate in a gap among the boulders immediately at its foot. When the river begins rising after a drought, you can see them, a mass of thick blue bodies and waving tails, waiting for the water to rise sufficiently to let them run up.

When it does rise, there are two ways up the big fall; one straight up over smooth sloping rock, while the other is a natural fish ladder round a small heathery island. Only a fraction of the water flows this way, but the majority of the fish take this easier ascent, and join the main river again in a small pool immediately above the big fall. Here they rest for a while and take well. You have to wade up to your knees, through a glide of water over smooth rock, to get in position below them. You cast your worm up into the welter of white tumbling water of the fall above, and it is washed down into a small ease beyond the main current. The worm stops, with a series of firm tugs, and you strike. Then anything can happen because the pool is too small to play a sea-trout bigger than 1lb. As soon as he feels strong pressure a larger fish turns and tears back down the main fall in among the great tumble of boulders below. You have to get ashore and hurry after him as best you can.

One of these days I shall probably fall down and hurt

myself, for one tries to follow as fast as one did thirty years ago. I should have done so already had I not discovered an alternative to rubber boots called NORAS which don't slip nearly as readily on wet rocks. A 3lb. fish can easily take you a hundred yards downstream.

One day, when the river was very big and I had only just managed to wade out, I felt a fish take that I judged to be larger than usual. I handed the rod to Edward, who was on the bank, and told him to tighten. When he did we found that we had hooked a 5lb. sea-trout. With the greatest possible skill he kept it in the pool for quite a long time. He pulled it hard only when it was near the top of the pool, and eased the pressure when it got near the tail. When it became tired and eventually left the pool, he managed to steer it into the glide I had waded across. He held it for a second, and I, who was behind it by now, was able to scoop it out with a landing net.

It is always a happy party that walks back down the river and across the park to the house, usually carrying a netful of fish.

It is the uncertainty which is so exciting; you never quite know what will happen. Last year Brenda was fishing the falls pool with my brother Maurice, when she hooked what she thought was the bottom. She handed him the rod as he was on the bank, so that he could go round above and dislodge the hook. When he began pulling it began to move, and something sailed slowly round the pool twice and then got off. Apparently it felt like a tree stump; but then there are no trees in the Camasunary valley. What was it? Probably a salmon of about 20lb.; we once caught one of 18lb. in the loch, and perhaps we shall again one day, but I wish that one in the pool had held on. I expect it would have run the mile downstream to the fisherman's pool, if not right back to the sea.

6

SEA-TROUT IN THE SEA

EVERY EXPERIENCED FISHERMAN has one particular
place which means more to him than any other; he has
one kind of fish which he prefers to fish for. My place is
the island of Skye, my fish the sea-trout.

You fish for them with trout tackle, and you may hook
one of any weight from ½lb. to 12lb. The uncertainty is
much of the fascination. But whatever their size they play
better for it than a salmon. When you hook one he is off
with a tremendous rush, usually ending with a jump.
You then see the prize, perhaps the most beautiful silvery
fish there is, and the thrill is on. He will fight to the very
dregs of endurance, and at the last moment the hook may
come away if you pull too hard in your excitement, for
his mouth is soft.

Sea-trout on the west coast of Scotland only go to the
sea for a short time each year. During the winter, after
spawning, they hibernate, as do brown trout in northern
rivers where there is no food to be found. In the spring,
when the natural food in the water increases, they are
stimulated to go and look for more in the sea. It is then
that spates are needed so they can reach the sea and start
getting in condition. The annual growth rate in Skye is
about one pound per year. If there is no rain in the late
spring you may still catch kelts in the lochs in July, and
others at the river mouth where they are feeding like mad
trying to make up for lost time; but this seldom happens,
for there is usually plenty of rain in Skye.

When they get to the sea they don't go far away from their rivers. They are not caught in the bag nets off the coast of Skye and they suffer no dangers from the Greenland coastal fishermen or the deep-water drift netters, and so they will survive in quantity when salmon become scarce.

When they make back towards their rivers and lochs they continue to feed in the estuary while waiting for a spate, and they feed also throughout the autumn in fresh water. This means that by observation it is possible to predict their taking habits—and catch them.

Sea-trout run up every river and burn round the coast of Britain where there is free access to and from the sea and no pollution. While practically every salmon river has been developed as a fishery, there are still many sea-trout burns which are seldom if ever fished. People will travel to Norway and pay hundreds of pounds to catch one salmon, and although salmon fishing is less expensive in Britain than in any other country—if you can get hold of it—by comparison sea-trout fishing is still quite ridiculously cheap.

And what of the places where one goes to fish for sea-trout? In pursuit of our sport we see many lovely views, but usually one holds our particular affection and we can recollect every detail of it, smelling the clean fresh air, the scent of bog-myrtle in the sun, the distant tang of the sea. We can hear the absolute silence broken only occasionally by the sound of distant falling water brought on the warm wind, the cry of an oystercatcher or the breaking of a calm sea on a beach. We can walk in imagination on the path to the river and remember every rock, every boggy place and how the scene changes with each step. We can take friends with us, be children again with our parents, or walk with our own children.

Every one of us can find this, his own special place, but nobody has an exclusive right to it. Each place can be shared and hold the yearnings of countless people. I like to think that Camasunary in Skye means much to the many folk who have stayed there in the last 50 years, and I believe this to be so.

But there are many such places to be found by the eager young fishermen of today. There are few roads in the Western Highlands, but many small rivers and burns running through little valleys into the Atlantic. Years ago people lived in these valleys and you will still see the ruins of their scattered crofts. Now many of the streams are miles from the nearest road, and if you visit them you will see only sheep and deer and sometimes a shepherd. Rivers by roads are all heavily fished, but many of the remote burns are never visited by a fisherman. Don't expect to be allowed to fish where other people are already doing so, but get a map and explore. Find some remote burn, where it appears that nobody ever goes. You may not have to go very far because as a nation we are losing the use of our legs. Nowadays few people leave a road, and only a tiny percentage of the visitors to the Highlands are interested in fishing.

When you have discovered a possible place, find out to whom the fishing belongs, and after shaving off your beard, if you have one, ask politely for permission to fish there. Also remember that you must always ask permission to camp if you wish to do so.

The older generation like good manners and cleanliness, if they are giving lifts or granting a favour. If you remember this more than likely you will be lucky and receive permission. This may be the last generation with these opportunities; very soon even the lonely Highland valleys may become crowded and developed.

Walking in the Highlands, if you like remoteness and beauty, is a joy in itself. But if you are a fisherman and carry a rod, with a purpose, it adds a spring to the step which eats up the miles tirelessly. The first visit to a new stream is perhaps the most exciting, but there is great pleasure in revisiting a known place. You will get to know it under all weather conditions and at different heights of water. Gradually your knowledge of where and how to fish will increase, and with it your chances of success.

Perhaps you will leave your car on a remote track and walk some way before the sea comes into sight. A tiny burn will join you on your journey, trickling among its pebbles. As you continue on your way other little burns will add their waters to it, the valley will widen and the heather beneath your feet will give way to green grass and rushes.

As you get nearer the sea there will be a few small, deep pools joined by trickles of water in fine weather, or by rushing torrents in a spate. When the river is low the surface of the pools will be calm but for the ruffle of the wind, and even under these conditions, if there are sea-trout, they can be caught there. If nobody else has fished for them, the chance of success is much better.

In fine weather and low water there is a place you should investigate before you start fishing the river: go right down to the mouth of your burn, and look at the sea. If you have had a long hot walk you will need a rest, so sit down for five or ten minutes and do the same as the thousands of holiday makers on England's crowded beaches, gaze out to sea. The only difference is that you will be looking for something.

If the tide is out there will be a stretch of shingle and a fringe of floating seaweed between you and the water. At first the sea is confined by rocks, cliffs and headlands, then it escapes and stretches away to distant blue islands and the infinite horizon. Let all this unspoilt and beautiful scene, which the old inhabitants must have loved so well, flood over you, but just keep an eye on the sea immediately beyond the fringe of seaweed. Quite soon you may see a sea-trout, and another jump within casting distance. For a while the scenery must become a background to your conscious thoughts.

You really need waders, but on your first visit you won't have any. Take off all your clothes below the waist, roll up your shirt tails under your woolly, put your shoes back on your bare feet, and get after those fish. The sea will be much colder than you expect and it will take your breath away as you wade out and it inches its way up over your warm white skin. You will have to wade up to your waist, and as you gradually get deeper there is one moment which is worse than the others. The seaweed feels coarse and rough against the skin; but soon you will be within casting distance of a jumping fish and all else will be forgotten as you get the line out.

Whatever you do, don't try this at the mouth of a prolific and protected river. The owner of the fishery has the exclusive rights of fishing for migratory fish for one mile out to sea. But if you have permission to fish a burn or river this will include fishing in the sea. Quite a few people fish for sea-trout in estuaries, but not many fish actually in the open sea. It can be the most exciting and rewarding place to fish, but here sea-trout are unpredictable in their feeding habits, and they alter from year to year. This is because the food pattern in the sea constantly changes. To become successful, observation on many occasions over the years is of the greatest assistance. You also need much practical experience of success and failure with various lures and baits under many different conditions before you can make the most of your opportunities. I hope you are lucky on the first occasion, for this will encourage you to continue.

At Camasunary, in Skye, the shoals of sea-trout congregate at the river mouth from the end of June onwards. If there are frequent spates you don't see very many as they run up the river at once, but after a week's dry weather you see them jumping in large numbers. At first most of the fish are big ones and you seldom see finnocks in any quantity until after July 20th; from then on the majority of fish which collect in the bay are finnocks,

although there are a few larger fish as well. They keep in
shoals during the day. The average weight of the fish
varies from shoal to shoal, the bigger fish seeming to keep
together as do the rather smaller ones. They are most
likely to take when they have newly arrived in the bay and
are still feeding hungrily on the small fry which often
come close in shore in their millions when the weather is
warm and settled. The longer they have to hang about
waiting for a spate, the less easy they are to catch. Nor
will they wait about indefinitely. After a while the whole
lot can leave the bay for several days but they will
probably reappear on the next spring tide and certainly
if there is a spate.

At high tide they will often penetrate as far up the tidal
part of a river as they can swim. They are most likely to do
this in the evening on a spring tide when they have newly
arrived. Here they will be very concentrated, and easily
covered from the bank, but although you cast a fly over
a great many fish they can be disappointing takers. They
are thinking of running, not feeding, when they enter
the river mouth.

At high tide the fish move very little and you seldom rise
anything. When it starts to ebb strongly the fish will drop
back and others may even appear. If you cast over them
they may follow the fly, and occasionally one will take,
but it is usually a small one.

Once they get out to sea again they will think of feeding,
and start taking. I prefer to fish the flood from about an
hour after low tide for the next two hours, or the ebb at
about half tide. But fish are always unpredictable in the
sea, and you must keep an eye on the water at all times.
If you spot them jumping, go and fish for them at once;
they may hang around for an hour or so, but are unlikely
to do so for much longer.

I remember one evening, just after high tide, when
great numbers of fish appeared practically in the surf off
a sandy beach. Some were quite red from waiting to run

5 Playing an autumn salmon

6　Landing at Scavaig to fish Loch Coruisk

up, when normally they are bad takers. Many were within easy cast from the shore without wading, and they took a fly surprisingly well. Sport was fast and furious for a while.

If you keep watching a bay you will notice after a while that there are one or two places where fish seem to appear most frequently. These are the places you should fish. Don't try to pursue a shoal if it is jumping out of reach. Wade out into position within cast of where they most often jump, and wait for them to come to you. Try a cast from time to time even if nothing is showing, but don't tire yourself by fishing all the time. A shoal of sea-trout practically always gives away its presence by one or two jumping, if it is near enough to the surface to be interested in a fly.

During the day at Camasunary the fish usually congregate over the shingle off the mouth of the main river, and off the mouth of a burn at the other side of the bay. These two spits of shingle are joined by a crescent of sand some three hundred yards long. If you wade out as far as you can, fish often come within reach. You need long waders and you mustn't forget the tide.

I lent Michael a rather doubtful looking pair of waders last summer, which had been left behind by Bobby. He waded boldly out into the sea and started fishing. About half an hour later there was an awful yell: 'Stevie, these bloody waders of yours leak.' I thought it strange that they should start leaking so suddenly and said so. A minute later rather a contrite voice said, 'Oh, hell, the tide has come in over the top.' He had done a Canute.

It is probably better to fish from a boat, if you can get hold of one. You don't then have the feeling that the fish are always just out of reach, which all fishermen know so well. If you are alone, anchor yourself in about 5 or 6 feet of water and in the centre of the spot where the fish show most frequently. It is terribly exciting when you are in position and see a shoal coming towards you. You can tell

E

which way they are going by the way they are facing when they jump.

Now comes the question, how and with what should you fish?

It is always great fun experimenting when fishing, and I never cease to do so. Over the years when fishing for sea-trout in the sea I have tried practically every spinning bait, lure and fly that has ever been invented. The spinning baits I like best are a blue and silver minnow and a small Mepps spoon, but the latter is very light and consequently difficult to cast into a wind. When you fish for sea-trout with a spinning bait, you seem to hook a smaller percentage of the offers you get than when fishing with a fly or non-spinning lure. You also lose more of the fish that you do manage to hook.

I now believe that the best thing to fish with, from the point of view of catching the most fish, is a fly rod, a floating line and a three hooked silver lure. But if you cover a number of fish and none take the least notice it is well worth trying a spinner; it does sometimes catch a fish when a fly won't. Half the secret of success is to get whatever you are fishing with over a shoal of fish without delay, because they don't stay in reach for long. In this respect a spinning rod is a disadvantage. If a large fish jumps within reach, but in another direction from your last cast, it takes some time to reel right in and cast again. In the excitement of the moment I am usually hopelessly inaccurate when casting a light bait with a spinning rod. With a fly you can whip it off the water and smack it down on the fish's nose in a second.

Any silver-bodied fly like a Butcher or a Teal and Silver will catch fish. A sole-skin lure was very effective at one time. When the fish have been particularly tiresome, I have even tried tying a piece of the skin from a sea-trout's stomach to hooks, thinking that perhaps if it smelt of fish the sea-trout might take, rather than just follow it. It didn't make the smallest difference and was difficult to attach securely to a hook with tying silk.

The lure I now use is very simple and effective. It consists of three fairly small and very sharp sea-trout-size hooks whipped one behind the other to nylon; the overall length is about 1in. The hooks are covered with silver tinsel. On the front hook I tie three hackles as a wing; a scarlet one in the centre, flanked by two creamy white ones. Any other combination of hackles or wings can be effective, but I do like a combination of silver with some scarlet. The fly I have described is simple, quickly made, and it looks quite like a small fish in the water.

It helps if you can cast at least 20 yards and keep the fly moving for as long as possible by recovering it to within 5 yards of you. The line has to float in coils on the surface of the sea, or lie on the bottom of the boat, until you shoot it again with the next cast.

If a fish jumps within reach it is almost certainly one member of a shoal of anything between twenty and a hundred sea-trout, so absolute accuracy of casting is unimportant. But try to land the fly just in front of them. I used to recover the fly very fast, so it would look like a small startled fish trying to escape. This usually evokes a response, and bow waves appear from several directions and converge on your fly. There may follow a savage wrench and a flurry of foam as a fish turns and jumps. But very often there is only a tweak, or the fish follow along a foot or so behind the fly making no attempt to overtake it. You can see them in the clear water when they get close; then they see you and turn away. The next time you cast over that particular lot of fish one or two may show some interest, but they quickly get bored and pay no more attention.

When to strike is a problem if fish are tweaking and turning at your fly. If one misses and you strike you may snatch it out of the mouth of the next one waiting to have a go. One method is to keep the rod top pointing at the fish and go on pulling in the line until one hooks itself. This is all right up to a point, and you will hook more fish up to 2lb. by this method than by keeping the rod high and striking. But one day a 6lb. fish will take and break your 10lb. nylon with a savage tug.

Recently I have been pulling the fly in rather more slowly and steadily, and I believe you hook more fish this way. You don't see those exciting bow waves as the fish chase the fly, yet quite suddenly and unexpectedly there comes a tremendous tug. Fish seem to stalk up on the lure and take it much more firmly. The first time I tried this method was when anchored in a boat by myself off the burn mouth. Not a great many fish were about, although a few jumped quite close from time to time. I never saw the first one that took; quite unexpectedly there came a wrench at the line and I was into a 4lb. sea-trout. I managed to land him and ten minutes later I hooked one of 6lb. Fortunately he went round and round the boat about 50 yards away, instead of going straight in any one direction. I could never have pulled the anchor up and followed him if he had. Both fish went over the top of lots of seaweed, but sea-trout never go into it deliberately to try to escape. In due course the 6-pounder joined his pal in the bottom of the boat, and a very bonny pair of fish they were. It is always such fun having success all on one's own and returning triumphant to the rest of the party.

I suppose food in the sea is so plentiful for sea-trout that they never need to feed for long to satisfy their hunger, and when they do start feeding your lure may be outnumbered many times by the natural food available. I have often seen a shoal start feeding some distance from the boat, chasing fry all over the surface. It may take two or three minutes to get within casting distance, and by then they have usually stopped. Then quite unexpectedly a day will come when you will be lucky.

One day there was quite a strong off-shore breeze. The sea was the brightest of blue under a clear sky, and the little waves sparkled in the sunshine. We were on our way by boat to Coruisk, but when we saw some fish jumping at the river mouth Michael and I began fishing for them. For once, every fish we cast over meant to have it. On three occasions we were both playing a fish of about 2lb. at the same time. We lost quite a number, but still ended up with eight fish in the boat, which we caught in the half hour before the tide got too low and the fish moved away.

I also like an onshore wind and a bit of a wave. Fish seem to take better, although they are not so easy to spot in a rough sea, also if there is a big sea or swell running they don't seem to come close in—and even if they did I shouldn't be there to fish for them. Never a good sailor, I find that sitting still in a rough sea is quite fatal.

When it is flat calm you can sometimes see a riffle on the surface when a shoal swims close beneath it. You see them dimpling the surface, and this is particularly noticeable in the evening when the light begins to fade. You often see monster fish jump, usually rather far out to sea, but just sometimes within reach. Then the excitement is terrific, yet you nearly always seem to hook a smaller one.

I have always felt that sooner or later someone would hook one of the really big ones and eventually Edward did. He wandered down to the shore by himself one evening between tea and supper, while I was chasing rabbits in the park with the dogs. There were a few fish showing so he waded out, cast a fly towards them and immediately hooked a monster. It went off at a great speed. He had no control whatever over it, and twice it appeared to be making for the island of Rhum, some 15 miles away. But each time it stopped and turned parallel to the coast when he could see the drum of his reel through the backing. Eventually he had it played and walked it back to the shore. There it lay among the gently breaking little waves, and he pushed it on to dry land with a foot. He appeared at the sitting-room window, highly delighted with himself, carrying a sea-trout which weighed exactly 10lb.—6lb. was the previous biggest. Shall we one day catch a 12-pounder?

Fishing for sea-trout in the sea is rather a specialised form of angling; nobody should imagine that it is easy. You must be able to cast a long line with speed and accuracy, into a wind if necessary, and strip it in smoothly and quickly right up to you. Then you must be able to shoot it all, or let it run when you hook a fish, without standing on it or getting it caught round a projection on the boat. But it is the best possible training for casting for a novice. He will soon be galvanised into becoming an adequate caster by the sheer necessity of the moment.

There is also quite an art in rowing a boat for other people to fish from. If there are two rods, only one must fish at a time. If they both try to cast long lines in any direction, they will become hopelessly entangled behind the boat. If this happens, be sure enormous sea-trout will start jumping all round you. They will be gone by the time the muddle is sorted out, and tempers—even friend-ships—will be temporarily, if not permanently strained. I like to be at the oars on these occasions. I try to get the fishermen just within reach of a shoal and then row away from it as the fish pursue the fly towards the boat. If one rod hooks a fish the other can come into action and try to catch another fish from the same lot. Sometimes if the boat is close to a large shoal you can order a 'broadside', and both anglers can cast, but they must remember to cast parallel to one another, or give warning if they see a fish jump off the end of the boat, and wish to cast for it. Then the other rod must stop fishing for a moment. The number of fish caught is no measure of the fun and excitement.

Now I find the sea so exciting, and so do Edward and Bob, that we seldom go to the lochs in the evenings if there is any concentration of fish in the bay. We find at Camasu-nary that the best place to fish in the evenings is off the sandy beach between the river and the burn. There are never any midges when you wade out into the sea even on the calmest evenings.

After a good dinner you put on waders and walk the 200 yards to the sea-shore. The sun is getting low and the islands are pale in the distance. The dogs are happily hunting rabbits in the bracken, fish are jumping all across the bay, and someone else is doing the washing-up. Could anything be more perfect.

Two or three of you can wade out over the firm sand, 50 or 60 yards apart. On a calm evening the fish generally come within easy reach, in fact quite often they appear between you and the shore. At first they still swim about in shoals, but when the light begins to go they disperse and become spread out right across the bay. As it becomes dark you often see them dimpling the smooth surface of the sea all round you.

Some of the fish you cast over take, others don't; but you all share in the excitement when anyone hooks a fish. A reel screams in the quiet evening, and there are mutters of suspense from the lucky fisherman. If all goes well he backs ashore to land the fish. You congratulate him if he is successful, and condone if his gentle words turn to wrath. You also warn one another when a shoal is moving along the shore, or a particularly big fish appears close inshore. If you are lucky each fisherman may catch four or five fish during the evening. There should be several of over 2lb.

Gradually the light dims. Features on the mountains fade in darkness, leaving only the jagged black outlines. The islands disappear for the night, and the horizon out to sea blends with the sky. Hinds and their calves come down to eat the grass just beyond the high tide mark, and watch you without alarm. The seabirds drift in on silent wings and settle on the shore to roost. They make quiet, comfortable noises as they go to sleep. The air turns cold after the heat of the day. You don't realise how cold your hands have become until you put one in the sea, and the water feels quite warm.

In July you can see to fish until well after midnight, then quite suddenly you feel cold and rather tired. You

can think of nothing nicer than a final whisky and a warm
bed, so you wade ashore for the last time, gather up your
catch and return to the welcoming light which shines from
the window of the house. Soon you are all back in the snug
little sitting-room, reliving the recent excitements and
discussing plans for the following day.

7

SEA-TROUT IN RIVERS

MOST THINGS THAT trout and sea-trout feed on naturally
are alive, and practically everything has some movement.
Small creatures that live in the water, like minnows,
shrimps and the nymphs of flies, swim through the water.
Worms, caterpillars, maggots and grubs which fall into
the water by mistake wriggle convulsively for a while when
they find they are in the wrong element. Flies flit about
before alighting on the surface and then struggle to take
off again. Nymphs, when they come to the surface, kick
and move when they are hatching and drying into flies.

So fish associate movement with something edible, and
any movement will attract their attention, especially if
they are hungry. They will investigate the cause, which
must look like the thing they expect to make such a movement, before they will take it confidently.

However perfect your imitation of a fly may be, it will
lack the attraction of the fly it represents if it doesn't
move. When fish are feeding on surface flies they will
occasionally take a motionless imitation because a real fly
may be motionless on the surface for a short while before
taking wing, or struggling to do so. But very often they
will persistently ignore the artificial while taking all the
natural flies passing over them. This is particularly so if
they have plenty of time to examine your fly. An artificial
fly is more likely to be taken by a trout where the fish has
a short horizon and the water is shallow, swift flowing and
popply. Then the fish has not time to criticise the un-

natural immobility, and the water imparts a dancing motion similar to that of a natural fly.

If your dry fly drags it will often excite a fish at first. Only when he follows it and sees that the motion is quite unnatural will he become frightened. If a fish ignores your dry fly, while continuing to feed on naturals, don't give up hope until you have tried one final ruse. Let your fly float past him until you judge that he can just see it out of the corner of his eye, then give it a tweak and let it remain still again. If he sees the movement he may well turn downstream after it and take a second look at it. If it then passes his scrutiny he will sometimes take it. Don't give it a second tweak when he is looking directly at it, whatever you do, or you will frighten him. Not only the pattern but the type of motion must pass the fish's critical scrutiny. One is no good without the other.

In rivers sea-trout are usually still to be found in shoals, whether they are running or resting in pools. In order to catch as many as possible you must find out where they are without delay. It is easy to waste a great deal of time on a strange river fishing pools where there are no fish.

If we return to the small river you have discovered in the Highlands, there will be nobody to tell you where the fish are usually to be found. This you must discover for yourself. If the water is clear enough you may be able to see the fish in the water, but you are most unlikely to do so before they see you, unless one happens to jump when you are looking.

Many Highland rivers are peat-strained, in which case you can't see into a deep pool, but in any case you don't want to frighten the fish by showing yourself. The best plan, if the river is low, is to fish each pool upstream with a wet fly and a floating line. Stalk each pool carefully from below and kneel on the bank. Cover all the water within reach, gradually increasing the length of your line. Recover the line by pulling it in, steadily and not too fast, until the fly is five yards or so from the rod top. The pattern of fly doesn't matter much, but I prefer a small Butcher or Grouse and Claret. If anything is going to happen it will do so when the fish first see the fly. This is particularly true with fish that have never been fished for.

I know of nothing more exciting and satisfactory than finding sea-trout in some remote pool where nobody else ever goes. There are infinite possibilities in every deep, still pool bounded by banks of peat and rocks. When you cast a line it sends the gentlest of ripples across the calm surface of the water, you begin recovering the fly, when suddenly there is a swirl; you strike instinctively and the calm is shattered by a plunging sea-trout. Ten to one you have found a shoal of finnocks, but perhaps containing some fish of 1lb. or bigger.

You can't strike too quickly once you see the swirl made by a fish turning. They often only hold the fly for less than a second. When you have landed or lost the first fish, you need not wait long before starting to fish again. You will often move another fish a foot or two beyond where you rose the first.

In small pools it won't take very long before you have had all the rises you are going to get to the wet fly. Even if you rest the pool for an hour, and then try again with a wet fly, little if anything will happen unless fresh fish have come into the pool. But if you try fishing with a dry fly you will probably start rising them again.

I find dry flies most effective in a low water, on pools with little if any current. I don't think it matters if the water is calm but perhaps a gentle ripple is to be preferred. I use fairly small flies in three patterns; a Claret and Black, a reddish fly like a Soldier Palmer, and a grey fly tied with a badger hackle. I put two hackles on all my dry flies as it makes them float higher in the water, which is important. Fish may rise best at any one of these patterns. A change of fly is always worth trying when they become tired of what you are fishing with.

To hook finnocks with a dry fly you have to strike

extremely quickly the very second you see the dimple and the fly disappears. If you are quick enough the fish will be hooked in the tip of the nose.

If the strike comes too late you will feel nothing, although the fly will be thoroughly soaked.

I think one's reaction should be slower with a big fish. If there is one about he will very often be the first to rise, so I try to be more deliberate when striking at the first rise I have. Once you have found that only finnocks are rising, you can test your reactions against the speed with which they take and spit flies out again. The fish will win about five times out of six.

You can be successful with a dry fly in quite an appreciable current; but in a big water or a strong current, a wet fly fished downstream is usually much more effective. Try fishing a wet fly upstream and downstream under varying conditions to find when it is best to switch from one to the other. I fish a fly downstream in the same way I do for salmon, letting it swim naturally through the current and recovering it through the slack water on my side of the stream.

Some pools fish best upstream in low water, others downstream in a spate. This you can only discover by experience. After you have finished rising fish with a fly in a spate, it is always worth trying a Mepps spoon or a small minnow. You will sometimes hook a real whopper that wouldn't look at the fly. In an enormous spate I have known sea-trout refuse to look at a fly altogether.

Sometimes it really does rain at Camasunary. One year we left a bucket outside the door. It was filled to the brim in 36 hours. The black rocky hills below the racing clouds were streaked by sheets of white foaming water, the roar of waterfalls filled the air, the river was one enormous raging torrent with no sign of a pool anywhere. We tried a fly in every bit of quiet water we could find but entirely without success. Finally in the evening I took a spinning rod and cast a blue and silver minnow into an ease which is normally a backwater behind an island. I caught two fish each of 3lb.

Under normal conditions, and particularly when a spate is running in, a fly is more likely to catch fish than a minnow. I now seldom take a spinning rod with me; it is such a bore having two rods. You either have to put one down and go back for it, if you can remember where you put it, or learn to fish with one rod tucked beneath an arm. You can fish a worm with a fly rod, but very often fish will show more interest in a fly than in a worm in a reasonable sized pool where the fly can work properly.

Most west coast rivers have a series of pools at their mouths into which the sea comes at high tide. Very often the top one is a sea pool with a character all its own: it may be deep enough to hold sea-trout when the river is low and the tide out, but if not it will hold fish during a spate or when the tide comes into it. Yet although it may be full of fish, they are often difficult to catch. I have never had any success in them using a dry fly. Fish are still thinking of the things they ate in the sea, and take a wet fly best, fished down and across when the tide is ebbing, or the river is in a spate.

Tidal pools have a special fascination, with seaweed on the stones and tufts of thrift on the rocks, and that peculiar smell of rotting seaweed from the small stagnant pockets of water among the hummocks of grass. As the tide begins to creep up over the round stones anything may come in on it into the pool. Don't be surprised to see otters, seals, mackerel or salmon. When there is a spate, with fresh water thrusting far out to sea, all the waiting fish are attracted towards the river mouth. If they have been waiting for some time in the estuary, they will be eager to press on up the river; but as long as plenty of water runs and fresh fish are coming into the bay, some of the new arrivals will hang around the sea pool.

You can catch fish at any time of the tide, but my

favourite time is when the tide is ebbing and just leaving the pool. As the water becomes shallow at the tail of the pool you may see fish dimpling the surface right in the shallow. Start fishing in the quick water at the very head of the pool, because the biggest fish are often there. I once caught one of 7lb. right at the top of the sea pool at Camasunary. I fish with a Teal and Silver, Peter Ross, or a Butcher, and keep the rod top well up because a 4lb. sea-trout in quick water can take with a mighty wrench.

Half way down our sea pool, opposite a slab of flat rock, there is a spot where you often rise a salmon if there is one around. He sometimes misses the fly the first time, but you are in no doubt about what you have risen when you see that great swirling rise. Waiting those few minutes before trying again is agony, because he nearly always has it the second time.

Robin hooked a very big one there one day, but unfortunately he was fishing with a piece of nylon provided by my brother Maurice who thought he was only likely to hook finnocks. The fish made one plunging rush, flung itself in the air and that was the end. It later transpired that Maurice had picked the nylon up off the floor of the veranda, where it had lain in the sun for the last few years. Somewhat surprisingly they are still very good friends.

Always fish a sea pool right out. Fish often lie at the extreme tail of the pool. I think these are the fish which are not yet keen to run and they are often the most free takers. It is most exciting if you hook a large fish with the tide in, for there is nothing to stop him making for the open sea. The stones are very round and slippery, which makes running difficult.

If you rise and miss two or three fish, always check up that there is a barb on the hook. It is so easy to break a hook on stones when casting. You are never too old to do it either, and it is especially likely to happen if you are trying to cast rather a long line.

The sea pool at Camasunary is rather too shallow to hold

fish in a low water. The sea-trout always drop back with the tide; but one day we found a salmon of about 6lb. in it. The water was low and clear, and the larder rather empty. Edward tried for it with an upstream minnow. Twice the fish left its lie and followed the minnow, but it wouldn't take hold of it, so sterner measures were called for.

I covered the largest treble hook I could find with silver paper and lead, waded out within reach of the deepest part of the pool, and lowered it to the bottom at the end of a stout line with a strong rod. The tide was rising rapidly so Edward and Van guarded the bottom of the pool, and drove the fish back up to me when it tried to escape out to sea. A ripple made the visibility poor, and the fish had plenty of room for manoeuvre. I thought it was going to win, but eventually I struck when the silver paper disappeared beyond the fish, and hooked him below the jaw. It isn't nearly as easy to foul-hook a fish as one might imagine, and we were very fortunate to get that one. Contrary to popular belief it is usually much easier to catch a salmon fairly, as you will discover if you are ever tempted to try to poach one. Proficiency requires practice which I trust you will resist having. Unfortunately poaching the occasional salmon is terribly exciting, but you mustn't make a habit of doing it or it is no longer sporting or fun.

Every fisherman wants to catch large fish and this may become an obsession which removes all pleasure from catching small ones. You will hear people decry catching finnocks, or whatever the local name is for sea-trout the first time they return from the sea. They even refuse to call them sea-trout. This is such a pity, and these people miss so much fun, for, let us face it, nobody catches very many big fish.

Early during the season, in June and July, finnocks are small, and their flesh is pale coloured. They hang about the river mouth and estuary, often just beyond the seaweed fringe. Some run back up to the lochs when still very small. But by the middle of August the ones that remain in the sea have grown. They average over ½lb. (much bigger than most of the herrings you buy from the fishmonger), their flesh is now bright pink, they are very good to eat, and the most sporting fish for their size to be found anywhere.

If you fish a west coast river during August when a spate is running in, you can have the day of your life. Every pool may be blue with fish, and fresh shoals will constantly be coming in. There is a freshness in the air and a sparkle all around as the sun appears again.

So much of the time one spends fishing is unrewarded. Be thankful if a day comes when you can catch as many of these sporting little fish as you wish, in wonderful secluded surroundings. There is no point in keeping more than you need. Thereafter you can just keep the occasional bigger fish which you will catch from time to time. Every sea-trout has to start off as a finnock, and who knows, you may be releasing a fish you will meet again some day.

Finnocks fresh from the sea are the most free rising of any fish there are. What a pleasant change from the surly brutes one usually casts for. They are perfect for starting children to fish. You don't have to be able to cast at all well. If there is a good run in the pool any imperfections in casting are soon straightened out. The smaller the child the less far he need cast for he can go closer to the fish without being seen; he will certainly have lots of pulls, and with any luck he will soon be learning how to play his first fish, as a fat half-pounder, never to be forgotten, jumps its way down the pool. There is nothing like success for making the young into keen fishermen. A boy coming back from the river, which he has been fishing before breakfast, with a net full of half a dozen silver little fish should himself be hooked for life.

Fishing a sea-trout river by day, when a little trickle of lukewarm water runs between still pools, is usually a waste of time. It is far better to avoid frustration and go willingly on expeditions with the children or girls, who seem to adore the sun. You may even catch mackerel and lythe, which can be great fun.

After dinner is the time to go fishing. The sea or a fresh-water loch may be the best chance of catching something; but when the light fades someone should try the pools in the river where there are known to be sea-trout. I like to start operations when it is just too dark to see where the fly is falling. Then sea-trout can no longer see you against the bank, nor are they the least scared by a fish rushing up and down the pool. As soon as you have landed one, and the commotion has died down, you can start fishing again in the same place, and hook another fish immediately.

The pool at night is a quiet and mysterious place, when you can no longer see where the reflection ends and the rocks begin, nor the details of the hill beyond. Even if you know every foot of the bank you must be careful how you walk. The fish, which by day inhabit the deepest part of the pool, will be spread right along it, from the trickle of a run at the top to the shallows at the tail. They move about quite a lot at night, and you can see great waves reflecting the light from the sky as they swirl and turn in the shallows.

I use an ordinary wet fly that looks like a moth, or a silver bodied Demon tied on three single hooks. Always take a torch for changing a fly; but also remember that it makes one terribly blind for a while afterwards. A really calm night is best, but don't forget to take the fly repel-lent. Midges on a calm summer night in the Highlands can make you frantic and drive you from a pool teeming with rising fish.

I have tried nearly every preparation that has so far been produced and have a standing order with two chemists for each new one that is brought on the market. Not one of them lives up to the advertisements on the outside of the tube. They may work with mosquitoes in Finland, or black flies in Bulgaria, but the midges of Skye are made of sterner stuff. Any preparation is, however, better than nothing. They stop the midges from actually biting. If put on thicky enough, the midges get bogged down as they crawl about looking for a spot you have failed to anoint where they can bury their wicked fangs.

If you have no repellent, and you are driven home, your worries are only just starting. Each one of those innumerable bites will begin to tickle at about 3 a.m. Then you have to systematically scratch them all in turn until they bleed before you can get any rest. This performance is repeated twice nightly for at least a week.

This at least can be prevented if you use an ointment made by May & Baker called Dibrogan. It is miraculous for any spot, stopping pain and swelling and clearing it up in a day or two. If the doctor or chemist know nothing of it, get some from your vet.

But let us return to the pool and assume you can stand the tickling of the midges' tiny feet. Start fishing right at the top, where the quick water trickles among the boulders. You must learn to judge the length of the line entirely by the feel. It is no easy matter to fish a run a few feet wide in the pitch dark when you can't see the fall of the fly. Fish down and across the stream, and pull the line in quite slowly with the rod top held low. By so doing it is easier to feel the slightest touch. This is important because fish usually take very gently at night. Strike at once when there is any suspicion of a touch, never wait until you are certain or it may be too late. Use very strong nylon because you may well be striking into a fish of over 5lb., and with a rod held low and a quick strike the force is considerable. The ideal is to strike quickly but gently, but this is almost impossible.

Half way down the Fisherman's Pool at Camasunary there is a rock where you can rest your back. This allows one to relax one's body and it is surprising how this assists one's sense of touch in the dark. There is a slight hesitation and you strike. Very often the fish just bends the

rod and is gone again; but sometimes you are into something solid that goes off like a torpedo with the reel
screaming. At first you can only judge the size of the fish
hooked by the feel. If it is really solid, and you can't feel its
body move as it swims, it is probably over 4lb. A big fish
will explore the whole pool when being played, running
right down to the tail and swimming about among the
projecting boulders. It will then tear off up to the head
and do the same. It only has to get the line round one rock
and you will be broken at once. Running in the dark is
hazardous, but somehow one manages it, for one must
keep in close touch. As the fish tires it breaks the surface,
then perhaps there is a gleam of white in the depths of the
black water. Before starting to fish try to find a good place
to beach a fish, as it is almost impossible to use a net at
night by oneself. Very often it is only when it comes into
the shallows that one realises how big the fish is. The last
few runs are always the most anxious moments, but at
last he is safely ashore.

I have known fish take all night long, until the sky was
brightening in the east. On one memorable occasion we
caught seventeen weighing about 40lb. in one night, but
usually you only get one or two rises. The biggest I ever
caught was 7½lb., but I think there have been some bigger
ones hooked and lost. I know for sure that the people who
hooked them will never forget their struggle in the dark
and the sickening feeling, almost of unbelief, when the line
went slack. It is so much worse when there is nobody with
you to witness what an enormous fish it was. That fish can
have such a strong emotional effect on us humans is
extraordinary.

8

SEA-TROUT IN LOCHS

THERE IS ONE method of fishing for sea-trout in a loch with a fly which makes the fly appear completely natural. Watch how a daddy-long-legs skims over the surface just touching the water for a second every few feet. By dapping correctly, using the best modern equipment, it is possible to make an artificial fly behave in exactly the same manner. You can overcome the difficulties which the ordinary dry fly fisherman finds insurmountable, and, by imitating the exact motion of a live fly, draw fish to your artificial one from deep and far. It is the movement, not what causes it, that first attracts the fish's attention. He will see movement from far further off than he will notice a motionless floating fly. He associates movement in the water with food, and will find the desire to make a closer inspection irresistible.

The attraction of a dapping fly is such that you hear of people having fifty or sixty rises in one day. You also hear of those same people only hooking two or three fish.

When you look at the flies they use the explanation is simple. Most of these flies are huge and quite unlike any fly that ever was outside a tropical jungle or a nightmare. They attract fish by their movement, as would a shaving brush; but no fish in its right mind would dream of eating one when it comes near enough to have a careful look at the cause of the disturbance. The only time they may make a mistake is when there is half a gale blowing, and the waves are three or four feet high. Then they have no time for a critical survey. Their vision is confused by the rough surface and they must be quick or the fly will be blown away. So the gentlemen who go dapping pray for a gale, which makes fishing uncomfortable or even dangerous. They dislike calm or sunshine.

There is a very simple answer to catching fish on the dap when the weather is nice and sunny with just a light wind. You can still make the fly behave naturally with correct tackle. Why not make it look natural as well?

It is not necessary to be an exquisite fly tier to achieve success. It is hardly possible to produce anything less life-like than many of the dapping flies sold in shops. Most of the creations sold are twice the size of any natural fly that ever was seen in the Highlands and they have two improbable great tufts sticking out of their heads, like enormous hairy ears.

One day my boy asked what they were for, and I replied that I hadn't the smallest idea. 'Well, why not put them at the other end, they would at least look like a tail', he said. We christened the results Tod flies.

For me the perfect place to tie flies is in the veranda at Camasunary. The first thing I do on arrival is to set out my materials so that anyone can go and tie themselves any fly they fancy. Some of the materials can be found lying about in the ground outside. There are various shades of seagull feathers for wings of heather moths, and bits of sheep's wool for bodies. During a holiday you can make experimental flies and modify them as may seem necessary. I have now developed a fly which is quick and easy to tie, looks quite like a daddy-long-legs on the water and, most important of all, catches fish.

When you see a 'daddy' on the water, the impression is one of great lightness. Only the tips of its legs touch the surface film of the water. Some of its legs stick out behind it and some project in front. An imitation should not have the hook penetrating the surface film for this is just as unnatural as having tufts sticking up in the air.

I tie my imitations with the simplest of materials: grey squirrel tail and black-faced sheep wool. I put several strands of the fur out at the back, and depress them with the tying silk so that they project down and around the point of the hook. Rough grey wool makes the body, wrapped round the well-waxed silk. Projecting forward at the head, I tie a fairly big tuft of squirrel fur, which I secure with nail varnish, and divide into three with the silk. Two tufts stick out sideways for the wings, and one forwards and down for the front legs. The bits that go the wrong way are cut off. It need not be the least tidy, for whoever saw a daddy-long-legs that was, but it must be so tied that when it drops on a table, the hook never touches the surface. This is really the only fly you need, and I always start by trying it, although most of us like a change if the fish aren't taking.

There are two fairly large flies which are sometimes seen stranded far out on the surface of a loch—bumble bees and blue-bottles. On occasion I try rough imitations of about the correct size, tying a Claret and Black and a Soldier Palmer to imitate the bees, and a fly with a black hackle and dark blue wool body to imitate the blue-bottle. On both I put black hackles projecting down round the hooks to keep these clear of the surface. But this is not so necessary with these heavy bodied flies; they are not nearly as light on their feet as a 'daddy' is. When they fall on the water they often fail to take off again. They gyrate slowly, buzzing their wings, and parts of them may well go through the surface film of the water. While fish will take imitations when they are fairly wet, I think they work best when absolutely dry. Certainly when fishing with an imitation 'daddy' it is most important that the fly should be perfectly dry and right on top of the water all the time.

I gave Bob some of my flies to try on Loch Shiel last September. One evening the fish really came on to take. He hooked them just as quickly as he could play and land them and get his fly on the water again. The thorough drying and oiling of the fly took some precious time. He thought that as they were taking so well it couldn't really matter, so he tried fishing again when he had half dried the fly. He didn't get one more rise until he dried it properly and oiled it again, and then the fish took as freely as before. It was interesting that he didn't see a single natural rise, and he was the only fisherman who had any fish that evening, although there were several other boats out dapping.

Daddy-long-legs vary considerably in size, but as long as the fly you use is within the size limits of the naturals, fish will take them freely. They will even take bigger ones than natural in a big wave. A big fly sometimes seems to rise more fish than a small one, but certainly on a calm day fish take a small fly far better. What is the use of rising hundreds of fish if you can't hook them? Using my own small imitation 'daddies' one day I hooked six fish out of six rises, and five out of seven the next.

In the evenings heather moths appear and fly out over the lochs, often flopping on to the surface and making a commotion. When you see fish rising they are probably taking these moths. Certainly fish will go on taking a dapped fly for as long as you can see one, but when you have to fish entirely by feel, a wet fly pulled in slowly is the only chance of hooking a fish. The imitation 'daddy' seems to rise fish in the evenings. I have no special fly for imitating a moth—it might well be worth trying to tie one.

Success or failure and certainly pleasure when dapping depends largely on the tackle. The man in the shop will try to sell you a special dapping rod with off-set rings, and I am sure it is very nice to fish with. I use a 14ft. fibreglass salmon rod, which I find perfectly adequate.

The dapping line is the one essential part of the equipment. For many years floss silk was the standard blow-line. It had so many disadvantages that it was almost impossible to fish with it on our gusty lochs in Skye. A friend gave me some floss nylon which was infinitely better, but it was not on the market. Now at last the Norris Shakespeare Co. of Redditch are marketing a wonderful looking floss nylon dapping line called Fish Hawk, and if it is half as good as it looks it will do. It is very strong, easily dried by pulling it through paper tissues, and when not under strain it is beautifully fluffed out to catch the lightest air. (When using the nylon I was given before, you had to tease it out by hand). I use about 20ft. of blow-line attached to mono-filament nylon backing on my reel.

Alterations are required in the tackle and technique employed depending on the strength of the wind.

With floss silk a strong wind was essential to get the fly away from the boat, but with floss nylon it is possible to dap in an almost imperceptible breeze which barely ruffles the water's surface. Under these conditions the cast between the floss and the fly must be short and of fine nylon, say 3ft. of 4lb. breaking strain. A small light fly is also required. If there are other people fishing the same loch, they will think you mad to go out dapping when there is a flat calm, but don't let that worry you. You will have the place to yourself. When you feel that little puff of wind on the back of the neck the fly will float gently away from the boat, and alight like thistle-down on the calm surface. Then another little puff will come and move it a foot or two. At any moment a great head may appear and the fly vanish beneath the water.

On a very windy day the technique for dapping must be quite different. I think the fluffed out nylon blow-line may be at a disadvantage compared with a heavier one, as it will blow about so wildly in the gusts, but there are several things that can be done to control its exuberance. One is to use a long cast of heavy nylon, say 8ft. of 12lb. breaking strain, and the rod top is held much lower. In a big wave with a strong wind an anchor fly is also of great assistance. The dapping fly should be fished as a dropper, and two feet beyond it you have a heavy wet fly as a tail fly. When a gust comes, a dapping fly without an anchor goes all over the place, sometimes even vertically up in the air. With a fairly deep anchor it only goes a yard or two in a much more controlled manner.

Besides the anchor fly itself can easily catch a fish. On some days it may catch more than the dapping fly does. It must look most realistic as it darts here and there or remains motionless and slowly sinks, depending on the pull from the dapping fly. Certainly a fish which has been attracted by the dap and missed it will often take the anchor fly as an alternative. The first fish which Michael caught with us in Skye did just that. It had three goes at the dapping fly and missed. Eventually it took the tail fly, I suspect out of frustration.

If the wind drops somewhat I remove the tail fly but leave the trailing nylon as a slight brake on the dapping fly's activities. On a stormy day the strength of the wind is constantly altering; but you don't want to be forever changing the tackle. A fish can only take when the fly is on the water, and that is where the successful fisherman has his.

Very few of the things one does when fishing are original. I have not been dapping seriously for very long, and much of what I know about the technique I learnt from Michael or his father John. They are perfectionists, and both are highly successful on Loch Maree. I have found that their methods are equally effective in Skye. Any advice I give is based on practices which do work, and have proved effective over the years. Last year they gave me another invaluable piece of equipment, a rod holder which clamps on to the boat's gunwale. It is a tube into which the rod's butt slips and so remains vertical. Both the hands are then free for drying flies or changing the tackle.

Between the two extremes of a gale or a flat calm is the weather which I think is ideal for dapping. I like a warm day with a light, steady wind from the south, and quite a lot of sunshine. Most dappers dislike the sun, and Michael always groans when it comes out, yet on our deep lochs in Skye I am sure you rise more fish when it is shining. If the fly bears close scrutiny in a strong light there is nothing to fear from the sun.

The loch, where I should wish to be on such a day is Loch na Creitach, one mile north of Camasunary, where the water is the deepest blue. You first see the mile-long loch when the path tops a rise some 300 yards away. Beyond green grass and heather stretch up to the red granite masses of Marso and Ruastack. The black peaks of Blaven are on the right. To the left is the sheer ridge of Sgurr na Bannadich which divides the Camasunary valley from Loch Coruisk. The water is absolutely clear as it laps the smooth round stones of the beach where the boats are kept and soon your boat is drifting gently over the water with the dapping flies floating out over the rippling surface.

Try to imitate as nearly as possible the actions of a 'daddy' when it flits across the surface of a loch. If you don't know how he behaves catch some, let them go and see what they do. A boat drifting slowly makes a perfect imitation quite easy. Aim at keeping the fly just clear of the water when it is being blown out. Allow only the fly to touch the water's surface for a few seconds, and then move it on the amount the boat has drifted. Never let the floss touch the water, and dry it immediately if it does.

On the loch all is concentration and stillness except for the slightest movement of the rod tops. It is nearly as much fun rowing the boat as fishing, for you can see everything that goes on and watch both the flies. Soon three things will happen at once. A fish will appear; part of him must come out of the water to take the fly, and if the light is right you will see his brown shape in the clear blue water. The fly will disappear. There will be a disturbance on the surface of the water.

Fish rise to the dap in a number of ways. Perhaps the most exciting is when the fly is clear of the water and a fish comes clean out after it. Sometimes he takes it, but very often he misses, and you are faced with an angling certainty. When you put that fly back on the water, a few yards downwind, the fish will be round and after it at once, for it has behaved exactly as a natural would. This happened when Brenda was just letting her line out one day when we were all in the boat. The fly was more than a foot above the water when a fish of about four pounds rose but just wasn't tall enough to reach it. The two boys and I all shouted, 'Put it down Mummy.' This she did and the fish had it almost immediately. Unfortunately she wasn't organised and hadn't got a finger on the line. The reel had a very light check and when she struck it revolved without hooking the fish.

One day I must take a ciné camera with me to photograph fish rising to a dapping fly. By waiting for these moments very little film will be wasted.

When rising to flies that are resting on the surface, fish may just put the tips of their noses out and suck in the fly, or put most of their heads out. They can take with a very slow head and tail rise which barely disturbs the surface, or come with an almighty splash which frightens the life out of you.

A problem that is discussed around the bars of fishing hotels, or wherever dappers congregate, is when to strike. As most of the fish they rise never so much as open their mouths, there is much speculation and experimentation. If the fish mean to take, and they usually do if the fly looks natural, the problem is considerably easier to solve. Fishing with natural mayflies or 'daddies', you can and must wait quite a long time before striking. With artificials, which don't taste or feel right, you must not delay striking too long or fish will spit them out again.

When I started my eldest boy on dapping two years ago I told him to strike quite slowly, but he was much too

excited to carry out my instructions. He rose five fish and
struck the instant he saw anything. To my surprise he
hooked the lot, although they were all fish of 1 to 1½lb.
He then rose a fish of about 6lb. which he missed. Big fish
rise much more slowly and deliberately than do little ones.
The strike must be slower or you will probably miss them.
What is needed is one simple rule which covers all even-
tualities, and results in the hooking of a high percentage of
the fish one rises. What I do, and advise, is wait until the
fly and fish have completely disappeared again below the
surface, and then strike firmly at once.

If you try this and it doesn't work, by all means blame
me; but remember that there are days when fish rise to
a dapped fly with the sole intention of drowning it. They
don't even open their mouths, so however you strike they
won't be hooked in the mouth. They are sometimes foul-
hooked. After the fly is drowned the fish may return and
take it beneath the surface a few seconds later, so theoreti-
cally it would then be correct to leave it, and strike if and
when he does so. But how are you to tell that he hasn't
taken it in the first place? With only a fine bit of nylon
disappearing beneath the surface of the water 10 yards
away, I for one cannot see whether it is moving down
through the water or is stationary.

You simply must not strike if a fish is just nosing around
the fly. You sometimes see a fish doing this. The temptation to strike is great, but you must just watch the fly, and
only strike if and when it disappears. Move the fly a little
by all means, to make it look as if it is trying to escape
naturally, but if you strike it is very difficult to get it back
quickly in anywhere near the right place. To the fish it
will appear to move far too rapidly in the opposite direction to which the wind would have blown it.

I am all for encouraging beginners, and one advantage
of dapping is that a complete novice can learn in a few
minutes how to do it well enough to rise fish. As a result
quite a number of people who cannot cast a fly fish in this

way. Even people who can cast extremely well seldom seem to take a casting rod with them when they go dapping on a loch and this I am sure is a mistake. When I go out on my own I always take both rods. If fishing with a friend I am quite prepared to fish with whichever he doesn't want to use, until we see which the fish take best.

Sometimes there really is no wind at all for several hours, and dapping even with the lightest of tackle is impossible. If you have no casting rod you can't fish. Having travelled hundreds of miles to do so, the frustration will be immense. Going to sleep in a boat is most uncomfortable, and it is doubtful if you will be in a frame of mind to appreciate the scenery all the time.

If you have a casting rod in the boat, there are several ways in which you can fish. One is to cast a small dapping fly, and let it sit cocked up on the glassy flat surface. Every now and then it is advisable to give it a tweak to make it look alive. We have caught a great many fish in this way. When you get tired of looking at that spot, you cast again in another direction.

A wet fly will also often catch fish in a complete calm. If you cast it out and simply allow it to sink, fish will sometimes take as it does so; this is especially so in the evenings. To see when this happens you need a floating line, and must watch the knot where it is tied to the loop in the nylon. The moment this moves you must strike. If nothing happens as it sinks you can recover it slowly by pulling in the line as in normal wet fly fishing on a loch.

If you have a gillie it isn't really necessary to remain in the one place all the time, although it may be difficult to persuade him to do some rowing. Most gillies are pretty conservative, and nowadays consider that the boat should always be propelled by an outboard motor or the wind, never with oars. There is no earthly reason why he should not earn the enormous wage he will be getting by rowing the boat very slowly about the loch. Our gillies have always done this without complaint. If there are two rods fishing they row and back the boat alternatively, zig-zagging over the usual drifts.

Even if there is a dapping breeze the wet fly may catch more fish than the dap, but as a rule they are the smaller fish. One occasion when it pays to have both rods going is when fish are rising to the dap but failing to take a hold. If a wet fly is cast over them right away, they will quite often take it. A fish often intentionally drowns the dapping fly, and comes back to have a second look at it. If he finds your wet fly working slowly near the same spot it must look very like the fly he has just drowned, kicking and struggling to get back to the surface again. He wasn't sure if he wanted it the first time he rose, but may decide that he does now. One day Mark and Marjorie had considerable success in this way. Mark rose several fish to the dap, but failed to hook any of them. About half took Marjorie's wet fly, which she cast over the fish after they had risen at the dap, and refused to come again.

By day you nearly always rise many more big fish on a dap than you do to a wet fly. And you can entice them to rise in deeper water. Fish will come up to a dap in clear water fully 30ft. deep, whereas you seldom rise one on a wet fly in water much deeper than 20ft.

Dapping is undoubtedly more effective on some lochs than on others. We fish four lochs in Skye, all different in character. On two I prefer to fish with a dap; but on the other two I think you catch more with a wet fly.

While Loch na Creitach fishes very well with a dap, Loch Coruisk is not nearly so good. It is exceedingly deep and is surrounded on all four sides by precipitous mountains 3,000ft. high, so there is very seldom a steady breeze. This makes dapping difficult. One day last season however conditions were quite good, with a fairly steady breeze most of the day. I fished the dap, and Brenda a wet fly. She caught ten fish to my two. Admittedly they weren't big, only about ¾lb. finnocks, but I rose far fewer than she did, and never moved a large fish, although we catch some monsters in the loch at night.

I shall persevere however. One day they may take, for we have often caught them on a dry fly. The water is so clear that in a good light you can see them come right up off the bottom. On a sunny day in September fish often congregate in great numbers at the top end which is shallow with a sandy bottom. In a steady breeze a dap might be deadly.

Before we started dapping for sea-trout we caught most of our large fish on a fly at night. But you can't expect a gillie to row all night as well as all day. In July fishing with a wet fly by day was usually ineffective, so in fine weather we reserved our energies for the night. The gillies never seemed to mind being out all night if they had the day off, perhaps because they were three miles from the nearest girl.

I suspect that little night fishing is done on Highland lochs partly because of the difficulty of getting a gillie to row. It is almost essential nowadays to learn to row and work an outboard motor oneself. It makes one much more independent, and enables one to go fishing at any time. If I have friends with me I would just as soon row as fish. When you have fished a loch all your life you know just exactly where the fish are most likely to rise, and if they do when you are rowing, it is most satisfactory.

Night fishing is a fine-weather sport. If there is a good spell following a spate, there will be two or three nights when for a time the fish will take at almost every cast, but if the temperature of the water gets too high, they will go off completely. The best time to fish in early July is between 11p.m. and 1a.m. As the year progresses, and the nights darken, you must fish earlier. By mid-August 9p.m. to 11p.m. are the best hours.

Loch Coruisk must be one of the most wild and beautiful lochs in Europe. On a fine calm night as the light fades the mountains merge with their reflections in the water, and rise from the shore, like black curtains, to their jagged summits. A ripple on the water may reflect the light from the sky, otherwise the surface beneath those great cliffs is black as ink. Even the enormous glacial perched boulders round the loch's edge merge with the background. Utter silence covers the deep valley.

Fish tend to keep in shoals and move nearer the shore at night. The boat must be rowed along close in without a ripple or sound and the fishermen must be able to throw long lines to land lightly on the water, with no assistance from the wind. As you can see nothing, you depend entirely on feel to tell you when a fish has taken. Fish often just suck in the fly on such a night, so it is essential to recover the fly fast enough to feel when this happens. The moment there is the slightest indication of a check to the fly you must strike; that tiny touch may well be an 8-pounder, and if you hook him he will go quite mad.

Fresh-run sea-trout are great players, and there is nowhere they play better than in Coruisk. In a spate at high tide they can swim straight from the sea to the loch, and so preserve all their energy. This they expend the second they are hooked. They always start off with one tremendous rush of 60 to 70 yards and then give an enormous jump. You can just see a flash of white as a huge fish hurls itself in the air. Very often they get off as the strain on the hook's hold is tremendous, but sometimes they settle down and you can play them out.

A large salmon landing net is almost essential for landing a big fish at night. You can't see where he is, and must judge by the occasional break he makes on the glassy surface. Here the boatman can help by turning the boat to keep the fish in the most advantageous light. When rowing you have to watch the rod top all the time, to see where the fish is going and keep the oars clear of the cast. The man playing the fish must always be in the stern just beyond the oarsman, while the man with the net kneels right in the stern. After a while the fish begins to break

7   Loch Coruisk

8　Hand-lining for lobster pot bait: Brenda and the boys

the surface more often and nearer the boat. At last the moment comes when the net is lifted into the boat, and a great thick fish, white in the darkness, is yours at last. Then it is time to go home. The few hundred yards from the loch to the sea seems incredibly rough in the pitch dark. The smell of the sea comes on the night air, and there is the seaboat, a dark shadow on the grey water of the sheltered little harbour.

On the two miles home you have to steer by known features on the skyline to avoid the rocks in Scavaig as they are invisible in the shadows of the hills. The white phosphorescent wake from the outboard stretches back to the very heart of the Cuillins. Soon the boat rounds the last headland, and there is the light in the window of Camasunary House. When you get there the first thing to do is weigh the fish. Is it over 8lb.? If so, as it was caught on a fly, its outline qualifies for a place on the wall. But a place on the wall takes some finding now. The sitting room is fully decorated with various interpretations of what a sea-trout looks like, almost as varied as the works of art you see in the National Gallery. One actually is by a Royal Academician! The biggest of all, a fish of 15lb., is half-way up the stairs.

The best flies for night fishing vary from loch to loch. Perhaps a silver-bodied fly is best on Coruisk. Sometimes they take a three-hooked Demon. On Loch na Creitach I prefer an imitation of a heather moth, with a fluffy body, and a pale wing. A Black Pennel or Grouse and Claret are also good. It doesn't really matter very much what fly you fish with. If fish are on the go they will take anything within reason.

The bay on Loch na Creitach can be extremely good just after it has got dark, when the fish move right in close to the bank. Very often nothing happens until it is nearly dark, then suddenly they all come on to take. Both rods begin rising fish and no time must be lost as the rise may only last an hour. Strong tackle is essential to land fish up

F

to 2lb. as quickly as possible, while the other rod continues fishing. The object is to hook a big one in the limited time. If one of you does, the other rod must stop fishing at once and get ready to help with the net.

At night big fish usually play far from the boat, making an occasional break on the calm surface as they come up to it 50 or 60 yards away. But sometimes you hook one that seems to like to swim along in the shelter directly beneath the boat. If they do this the strain on a rod is tremendous, and it is extremely difficult to pull hard enough to tire them. It is easy to damage a split cane rod or break a green-heart when pulling hard at a fish directly beneath you. With fibreglass you can pull just as hard as you like with no ill effect.

One evening when I was rowing, Brenda hooked a fish that went to ground under the boat. She had fished for a number of years without landing one big enough to put on the wall, and had just been remarking on the fact when she hooked this fish. She was using a light 8ft. cane rod which was pretty old. It proved impossible to shift that fish from beneath the boat, where it swam along quite unconcerned; when I tried rowing away it followed, and I became more exhausted than it did. I could think of only one way to bolt it which was by rowing ashore on the gravel beach by the boat house. There were no underwater boulders there, and the fish had to swim out into the loch and play properly. We got it in the end and it weighed 10lb.—what a relief!

Lochs are not always calm. For days on end there may be gales of wind and torrents of rain, which often happens late in the season when all the fish have run up to the lochs, so it is no use fishing the rivers below them. It is too stormy for fishing from a boat, but there is one place where it is well worth trying from the bank. Fish where the largest rivers run into the lochs, and even in the bottom few pools of the rivers or burns themselves. The gale will make fishing into it impossible, and across it difficult. But if you can get the fly in the right place, and allow it to work across the waves, where the current meets the loch water, you may rise numerous fish. They won't all be small ones either. There is always a good chance of a salmon in such a place, or a sea-trout of 3 or 4lb. You see them clearly when they come to the fly, as a shape and a quick swirl on the steep side of a wave. When you strike they tear off into the rough water, with the line a great bow in the wind, and thrumming against the rod rings.

Landing a fish in such a place is seldom easy. Grass and heather at the water's edge are submerged deep beneath the risen loch and can entangle the landing net, dropper or taut nylon, but these fish usually mean to take and are well hooked.

Once you find out where they are you may rise fifteen or twenty and hook about half of them. So it is well worth braving the elements and walking a few miles even on the wildest of days.

There is no comparison between catching sea-trout on a fly or on a trolled minnow; but if they will take in no other way you may like to try trolling. Rowing round and round a loch all day is deadly, but if you have to get from one end to the other it is sometimes rather fun to see if you can catch a real big one. Sea-trout will take practically any of the spinning baits used for salmon. While I haven't sufficient experience to know which is the best, I usually try a blue and silver minnow or a Mepps spoon. A small trout mounted on a spinning tackle can be very effective on occasions.

Memories build up over the years, so you can shut your eyes and see the calm lochs or raging torrents; every detail of the towering mountain peaks. When I revisit them, and they are as beautiful as ever, I have to pinch myself to ensure that it is no dream. Knowledge increases for as long as one keeps trying new things. Skill, also, increases to a point where eyesight is not so good and limbs less active, but pleasure remains for as long as one is young at heart. I take comfort from the friendship of a man of eighty-five who has found the secret of eternal youth. He is as keen a fisher as when he was a boy, and takes as much pleasure in catching a perch, trout or salmon, as any man I have known.

9

SEA-TROUT IN IRELAND

EVERY FISHERMAN WHO has caught sea-trout in Scotland, and reads books about fishing, must want to go and fish for them in Ireland. Your fishing education isn't complete until you have done so. There is a magic ring about the word Connemara. The Irish are famed above all for their love of sport. I know that I longed to go to Ireland to fish from the age of fifteen, when I read about it in a fishing book I bought with the first prize money I won at school.

The other great attraction to Ireland is surely the Dublin Horse Show. What more wonderful holiday could there be than four days in an atmosphere where everything but the horse is forgotten, followed by a week in the West where sea-trout are caught in hundreds? That was my luck soon after the war, when one's zest for life was at its height.

Galway to me was the name of a famous hunt, and a bridge from which, I had read in my book, you could see countless salmon in the river below. The town itself is most attractive, but on arrival I hurried at once to that bridge. When I stood on it at last I knew that the author of the book had told the truth. There they were, rows upon rows of great salmon in clear view, complete with barbed wire below the bridge to stop the lads from having a go when nobody was looking.

The bridge over the Tweed at Kelso has no such deterrent, and sometimes in the autumn hundreds of salmon lie directly beneath it. To anyone skilled in the practice of poaching this must offer a sore temptation.

But the salmon at Galway are poached all right in spite of wire and bailiffs. I know a man—he had a garage near Darlington—who used to poach them as a boy.

Immediately above this long pool, where the salmon lie, is the weir at the bottom of Lough Corrib. Hugh and a friend had a canoe on the lough. On dark nights they used to go out together with a long-handled gaff and let the canoe right down on to the slap, where the water thinned and accelerated before the fall. It must have been a thrilling and risky business holding the canoe there in the darkness; just a little too far and they would have gone over—a canoe is never a very easy thing to manoeuvre even in daylight. Every now and then the smooth flowing water of the slap was stirred by the V of a salmon coming up from the river into the lough. Sometimes it was within reach.

Those two were never caught, presumably because the watchers never thought of anybody trying something as dangerous at night, nor were they swept over the slap, but I will wager they had some exciting moments when they got a gaff into a 20lb. salmon at full stretch of the gaff.

I did actually have a few casts in the pool with a fly. One of the rods fishing it was a lady who was a friend of my host, and she lent me her rod. When the bailiff appeared and asked me whether I had a licence, costing £2 for the day, I hastily gave it back to her. Anyway we had no time to waste and were soon on our way again, motoring to the West.

There are more boulders lying about in Connemara than you would think possible. Near the cottages they are collected into walls round tiny fields of the brightest green. Out in the open they are strewn all over the heathery moors. The shallow loughs are full of them.

At last we came to the final turning off the road. The track, just passable for cars, leads down a rough bank beneath overhanging trees and bushes to the very side of the Inver home lough. Suitcases and rods were put into a boat and we rowed 200 yards across to an island where the house is situated. In front of the house is a tiny harbour surrounded by hydrangea bushes in full bloom, 8ft. tall. The path to the very comfortable house leads up through a well mown lawn. The house had all that a fishing lodge should have; a library of fishing books, pictures of sea-trout on the walls; comfortable beds and chairs, and plenty of hot water; true Irish hospitality and the most palatable Irish whiskey I have ever tasted.

That evening, strange to say, the conversation was mainly about fishing. Local flies and techniques seemed to vary quite considerably from the methods I had employed all my life. I longed to test my own well-tried flies and ways of fishing which I have described in some detail in my first book, *Fishing From Afar*.

The landscape at Inver differs from the west of Scotland in that it is more undulating than mountainous. It is very difficult for a newcomer to get an idea of the lie of the land, and how it is drained. At Inver there are countless large and small loughs joined together by two separate river systems. On one such system there were boats on six of the loughs, on the other there were boats on two.

I woke early on the first day to find it was a calm sunny morning. There being more than an hour before breakfast I got up, took a boat from the harbour and rowed across to the foot of the highest hill I could see. It was about 300ft., but when I reached the top I could get very little idea of how the rivers ran, and it was not until I had had several days on different loughs that I got the hang of it. But it was a lovely sunny August day, and well worth the climb for the view: at my feet lay the home lough with its tree-covered islands and the rings of rising fish on the smooth water, in the distance the boggy, rocky moor stretched away and away with glimpses of lough and streams, all bathed in the clear morning light.

After breakfast I set out to fish a lough called Coreel. Although I was told that it was far too bright for the fish to take well, this did little to damp my enthusiasm, and I set off with the gillie along the path across the moor with a light step of anticipation.

The heat of the sun brought out the scents of bog myrtle and heather. Ahead the mountains of Connemara were blue in the distance. After a 2-mile walk we came to Coreel with its many rocky bays and heather clad islands. In Skye on a bright day I fish with a gold-bodied fly, so I decided to try one here. Soon we had the boat launched and we started a drift. On a strange lough every second the fly is on the water is one of the keenest anticipation. Sure enough after about five minutes there was a quick swirl and flash in the peaty water, and I had hooked my first Irish sea-trout. As usual I was fishing with my line greased, which enables one to strike just that second more quickly which is so important when hooking sea-trout with a wet fly on a lough.

At Inver they had very wisely put on a limit of 1lb. for sea-trout, and consequently I returned a number of smaller fish. We had many different drifts among the bays and islands of the lough, and lunched on one island where there is a charming little fishing bungalow. When it was time to return home in the late afternoon, I had kept five sea-trout. Perhaps it was not a great day's fishing, but one full of charm and interest.

After dinner I took a boat and rowed up the home lough to the spot where the biggest burn enters it. Further up this burn there are several small loughs, but they are pretty inaccessible, so they had put a grating at its mouth to prevent the fish leaving the home lough. This grating was removed in October to let the fish run on up to spawn.

As the sun set the wind died away, and it was very calm and quiet as I rowed into the little bay opposite the burn mouth. I ran the bows of the boat lightly on to a small rock just off the burn, and began fishing with a silvery Grouse and Claret. The only sound was the gentle murmur of the burn tumbling over the rocks into the lough. At about the fourth cast the line straightened, and when I struck, a fish shot out into the loch and took most of the line off my reel with its first rush. I hastily pushed the boat off and tried to follow, thinking it might be a salmon. However, it didn't go too far from the boat, and after a few more minutes I landed a very nice sea-trout of 4lb., which was a good size for Connemara. Soon it became dark, and I rowed home to bed content with a day I shall always remember.

If you tell an Irishman that you have caught a sea-trout of 8 or 10lb., he looks at you in total disbelief. And why should he believe you, poor fellow, when he has fished for sea-trout all his life in Connemara, and he knows that they are never bigger than 5 or 6lbs.? Naturally, being an Irishman, he is too polite to call you a liar, instead he begins telling you about the Leprechauns he has met in the west of Ireland.

I have not read any scales of Irish sea-trout, but presume the 5lb. fish there is about 10 years old, and the same age as a 12lb. sea-trout in Skye. In Ireland they must grow much more slowly, the reason for which must be that they spend less time in the sea, or find less to eat there than do our Skye sea-trout. In neither place is there sufficient food for them to grow appreciably in fresh water.

I only once discussed this matter with an Irish scientist, if the two can co-exist, which I began to doubt after a while. The discussion began on a highly technical and scientific basis, but deteriorated through time owing to his insisting on pouring large brandies into the coffee we were drinking after dinner in a Dublin hotel. Being a visitor and a guest I could hardly argue when he told me that in Ireland coffee was always drunk like that. But I can remember something of what he said earlier in the evening. He said that the feeding in the sea off Ireland was inferior owing to the proximity of the continental or Atlantic shelf. This is the line where the real deep water begins, and it is nearer the west of Ireland than it is to Scotland. But I don't suppose it is anywhere nearer than 10 miles from the coast, and sea-trout do not normally go that far out to sea. The proximity of deep water may however affect the feeding nearer the shore.

I feel that the probable explanation is a combination of several factors. Perhaps Irish sea-trout spend more time in fresh water, trying to feed when they are there, and spend less time in the sea, where they find less to eat than do our Scottish fish. This is rather borne out by the fact that Irish sea-trout certainly take an artificial fly very freely in fresh water. I do not think that the fish population of the Inver loughs was anything like as great as that of the Skye lochs, but they were very much freer takers. This may have been partly due to the water being more shallow, the average depth being 6 to 15ft. My impression was, however, that they feed more freely, and more often, in fresh water than the Skye sea-trout do. Whatever the reason, a different strain of sea-trout has developed.

This free-taking habit accounts for the enormous baskets of small sea-trout which can be caught in Ireland. One hears of many days when fifty or sixty were caught by one rod. There is no possible point in killing dozens of small fish in a day just to make an enormous basket, and it must contribute to the comparative scarcity of larger fish. At Inver they wisely had the size limit, which was raised annually, and the effect was already noticeable when I was there. They were catching far more fish of 2 to 3lb.

During my stay the weather was calm and bright for most of the time. I fished six different loughs and caught four or five keepable fish a day, and about twice as many under 1lb. which we put back. There was just one perfect day for fishing, dull with a good west wind. It showed me how easy those enormous baskets would be to catch.

It was August the 18th, and I fished Inver Mor with a wonderful ancient gillie called Pat. He hadn't much of the English that he was prepared to expend. When he rowed into the wind it was like being in the wake of a smouldering peat fire. They must never open a window in their cottages. He had rowed at Inver for over 50 years, and was reputed to know every one of the hundreds of submerged rocks in Inver Mor, which was his favourite lough. A few days previously, when rowing my host, he got the boat stuck on one. When he had pushed the boat off again my host said, 'Well, Pat, I thought you knew all the rocks in Inver Mor.' Pat replied, 'So I do, and that is one of them.'

He was a great artist at working a boat, desperately slow until something happened, but then he moved like lightning if it was necessary. We started fishing at about 10a.m.. I had a Grouse and Claret on the tail and my blue fly, with a dark blue wool body and a soft black hackle, on the dropper. The fish began rising at once, and they really meant to have it. If they missed they stayed around until they saw the fly again, and then had a second or even third try until they were hooked.

By mid-day I had caught twenty, of which we kept eight over the pound. The wind was rising and I began wondering whether the salmon in Lugeen might not be rising equally well. This lough was only half a mile away, much deeper and full of salmon, which were usually bad takers. After lunch I decided to go and have a try for them. It was a mistake, but large fish always have a special fascination, and a couple of salmon would have looked very nice among those sea-trout. I did indeed rise one, but in spite of my mental resolution I struck the fly out of his mouth. After that I didn't strike at all at the next dozen rises. Unfortunately, they were all from sea-trout, so I didn't hook any of them either, which was slightly frustrating.

We left Lugeen at about 5p.m. and I fished the drift back across Inver Mor. The sea-trout were still taking and I caught three more keepable ones. Towards the end of the drift old Pat suddenly said, 'If we stay here all day we catch twenty.' For a moment I wondered when the day officially ended in Ireland, and how hungry I should be by midnight. Then I realised that he meant, if we had stayed here all day, and I regretfully agreed with him.

I am always interested in local arts and crafts. When incarcerated in a prison camp in Germany we distilled our own alcoholic liquor, and the craft I was particularly interested in was the making of poteen in Ireland. Pat seemed very well up in it and after a while I managed to overcome his natural reticence. He then told me something of this fast-dying art. On the shores of the more remote loughs he would point out to me small thatched shelves where this ancient custom was still practised from time to time when 'the guards' were known to be fully occupied a long way off. Apparently, when distilling, the locals used no thermometer, an article we deemed essential in Germany and went to great pains to acquire from our captors. The Irish discovered whether alcohol was still coming over by throwing a handful of the distillate on to the peat fire. If it went bang they knew that it was still all right. But if it just sizzled it was useless, and they stopped collecting it.

I eventually asked Pat if he could get me a bottle to take home, and he said he might. The day I left he was waiting for me at the road-end with a bottle wrapped up in newspaper. It cost me 12/6. An inquisitive Customs officer was told that it was Holy Water, and so it reached England, and Darlington, where I was then staying, safely.

One day it was duly uncorked and a reek as of a peat fire filled the air. I tried an exploratory sip and it was just as if I had taken a red-hot peat into my mouth. It was undoubtedly potent but very, very nasty. It was the only bottle of alcohol I have ever owned that seemed to last for ever, and I kept offering it to my friends. It was still only half finished a year later when I left Darlington, and abandoned it in the cupboard. Shortly afterwards my nice old landlady died. I only hope there was no connection.

There can be no doubt that the experts are superior to the amateur when it comes to distilling alcohol. After this experience I was no longer so tempted to start my own home industry in Skye.

Yes, sea-trout fishing in Ireland is just as fascinating as I knew it would be. I can still see the delightful rocky loughs and feel the soft, soft air. One day I shall return there.

10

THE POT

I AM NOT going to attempt to compete with those great ladies of the cuisine, Mesdames Beeton, Spry, David and Prunier. It is, however, possible that I have gutted more salmon and sea-trout than any one of them, and my remarks are intended to help people who have caught fish and then wish to eat them.

When it comes to the point where you may wish to prepare a Court Bouillon, you must consult other authorities.

Salmon can be delicious to eat, or very nasty. There are many other factors, besides the cooking, which are responsible for this.

It would be difficult to encounter anything less palatable than the pale flabby piece of kelt I once met sitting on a limp lettuce leaf at a charity dance in a hotel in a Border town. I was sitting next to my hostess, and the charity was a noble one, so I ate it up bravely, pondering the while on what poacher had removed it from which burn.

Salmon are extremely vulnerable at spawning time, and shepherds in the Border hills spend many damp and exciting hours chasing them while evading the bailiffs. It must be a provision of nature that makes these fish practically inedible. Even the hungriest of shepherds tire of the sport after a few meals when they chew their way through great hunks of the stuff, washed down with strong tea.

Salmon usually taste as good or as bad as they look. A silvery spring salmon straight from the cold sea is a lovely sight. The first one you eat in the season, if properly prepared, is always quite delicious. But an old hen, all soft, red, and blotchy, just about to become broody in the autumn, looks most unattractive, and tastes little better than the kelt I met at that charity dance.

I am sometimes asked to smoke such fish, but I refuse because it doesn't do them much good. If you really must try to eat such a fish, Worcester sauce in liberal quantities is probably your best bet.

For good eating a salmon should be fresh from the sea; but perhaps it is more important that it should be several months before it will spawn. At the end of May and in June spring-run fish become rather coloured; but they are usually still very good to eat, because they will not be ripe for spawning before the end of October, or November.

The development of the reproductive organs seems to take the oil from the flesh, and change its texture and flavour. If you fish the Tweed in November you frequently catch split new silvery fish covered in tide lice. I have often been tempted to eat these fish fresh, but they are usually disappointing because they are nearly ready to spawn. It is almost always better to smoke them.

When eating salmon one's taste is easily satisfied and rapidly becomes critical. People who are in the fortunate position to catch salmon for most of the year seldom eat it as often as once a week. Those wretched apprentices probably did moan like anything: but isn't it strange that nobody has ever found a copy of that oft-quoted charter limiting the number of times they might be fed on salmon? You would think there must be one somewhere since you hear this story as coming from England, America and many other salmon-producing countries.

You don't get nearly as tired of eating brown trout or

sea-trout. My boys enjoy brown trout for breakfast all through the Easter holidays. After a fortnight in Skye, having sea-trout at least once a day, I always ask people who are staying whether they would prefer eggs and bacon for breakfast on the last morning. Invariably they ask for sea-trout.

Sea-trout from the west of Scotland are delicious up to the weight of 5 or 6lb. But as they get heavier and older they become rather less good to eat. By the time they are 12 to 15lb. the flesh has become paler, and they are much more fun to catch than to eat.

Once you can forecast how good or otherwise a fish you have caught is going to be to eat, you can consider what to do with the less good ones. Hotels will often buy them and feed them to unsuspecting or indeed appreciative bus loads of tourists. Friends 'in the South' who can seldom afford to buy salmon are less critical than the fortunate people who live on or near a salmon river. Finally, don't forget your mother-in-law and the 'old folks' homes'.

The fisherman has yet another indication of how good the fish he has caught is going to be to eat. The 5 or 6lb. sea-trout plays much better per pound than does a very large one. If a brown trout plays exceptionally well for its size it is sure to be good to eat; but if you hook a large one that comes flapping in almost without protest, it will probably be inedible.

Sea-trout from the Middle Tweed in the Autumn are disappointing to eat; but I am told that the ones from the Till in the spring are excellent. One October I caught a most lovely sea-trout of 5lb. below Galashiels when Brenda was away for a few days. I thought my cooking problems were solved: hot tonight, cold tomorrow and kedgeree and fishcakes from then on. After one mouthful I had to rearrange the menu. Even the dogs were a bit puzzled.

Some brown trout have pink flesh and some white. I don't think that it is much guide to flavour, although our appreciation is affected by our eyes, and many people prefer a trout with pink flesh.

The purity of the water is all important. Minute traces of some substances can make trout taste very nasty. Trade effluents can alter things rapidly, and make normally delicious trout quite inedible.

The Jed trout are white fleshed and particularly succulent, partly because there is little pollution in this hill stream; although when we came to live here, and I put in a septic tank, it was the only one in the entire valley. Shortly after the installation the County Sanitary Inspector landed up and asked why we hadn't submitted the plans to him. I suggested that his time might be more profitably employed by visiting and inspecting all the other houses that hadn't got one at all. He seemed rather hurt.

The flavour of trout in rivers alters from year to year with changing conditions. Tweed trout used to be very good, but have been pretty nasty, from where I fish, for the last few years. Local knowledge is all important before you can forecast how good a trout will taste. On all rivers a fat trout tastes better than a thin one, and the flavour improves as they get into condition during the spring and summer.

This also applies to trout in most lochs, although it didn't occur in one near here which was stocked with rainbows. They grew at a prodigious rate, fought like mad, and were wonderful eating early in the season. A month later we recommended them to friends, and tried eating some more ourselves. For some reason they had become quite inedible.

If you are keen on eating good food you soon learn to assess the eating qualities of the fish you catch from different places at different times of the year. I find that this makes a difference to my fishing plans as I get far more pleasure from catching small trout that are good to eat than larger ones that are not.

G

Catching trout, sea-trout or salmon is an important first step to tucking in the napkin and starting in on a delicious fish dish. The fisherman is at a great advantage over those people who must buy their fish, because he knows when and where his fish were caught. But knowledge of the keeping qualities of fish is also essential. There are many things that one must learn the hard way, but some unpleasant experiences may be avoided. One is the odour of decomposing fish. I believe that there is a Spanish proverb: 'Guests like fish stink on the third day.' As regards fish this must only be taken as a rough guide.

Salmon keep fresh for longer than trout or sea-trout. The reason for this is partly that their digestive system is no longer functioning when they enter fresh water, and partly that they are a different species of fish. But the consistence and quality of the flesh alters if they are kept. If you cook a fresh run spring fish on the same day as it is caught the flesh is very firm, and the fat in the connective tissue between the muscle is a hard white 'curd'. Some people consider this perfection. If the salmon is cooked on the following day this curd has turned to a soft oil, and the texture of the flesh become softer. I think the taste is then more delicate.

In the spring you can keep a salmon in a cold larder for 4 days; in the summer for about 3 days. In a refrigerator they can be kept for 5 or 6 days if necessary, but the fresher they are eaten the better. It is not worth sending salmon by post if their journey takes them through London. A few days' delay in a cosy post office does them no good at all.

Brown-trout and sea-trout are scientifically the same fish and keep fresh for the same length of time. Once they are killed they start digesting themselves, so it helps them to keep if you gut them immediately they are caught. But even if you do this they will not keep for as long as salmon at the same temperature. The length of time they do keep depends entirely on the temperature. They should never get hot, and it does not improve them to lie on the bottom of a boat, in full sunshine for half a day. The skin gets hard and the flesh very soft. When you get them home they will be smelly in 48 hours. If you visit the larder on a dark night and the sea-trout are glowing with phosphorescence this is a bad sign and means they will be stinking by next morning.

They should be kept as cool as possible after capture and gutted as soon as convenient. If they are put in a refrigerator the same evening they will keep for 3 days. At Camasunary we now have a Calor gas refrigerator which makes the world of difference for keeping sea-trout fresh over the weekend.

All fish will keep for ever in a deep-freeze, but their flavour is affected by being frozen solid. If you eat quite a number of fresh salmon you become very critical of any that are not quite perfect. I have never been satisfied by any that have been in my deep freeze, and I no longer put salmon in it. If you only occasionally catch quite a number of salmon it may well be worth preserving a few in this way. If you wish to do so I think you should freeze the whole fish as it comes from the river in a commercial deep freeze which employs a blast of cold air, and so freezes the fish very rapidly. You then cut off a chunk with a saw when you want to eat a bit. If treated in this way—and made up, i.e. not eaten plain—it can be nearly as good as fresh salmon.

I have been equally unsuccessful in deep-freezing trout and sea-trout. I have tried with specially selected fish in two different ways. One was in sealed polythene bags and the other in a block of ice. When melted out later they had all acquired a pale yellow tinge and a strong taste of rubber, goodness knows where from. Both these methods were recommended to me by friends, who presumably have taste buds in their mouths, so there may be some secret to freezing trout which I have not yet discovered.

We have had much more success with freezing cooked fish, like potted salmon and salmon mousse. Trout cooked in smoke also keep well

Smoked salmon, which is cured and not cooked, can be kept in a deep freeze; but the smoky taste gradually evaporates, and in time it becomes dry and hard. The outside also loses its colour and it becomes pale. I try not to keep mine for longer than 3 to 4 months. I cut it into convenient-sized pieces for a dinner party before freezing it in polythene bags. I slice it thinly just as it is thawing out. It is very easy to cut it as thin as you wish if you choose the right moment.

The wives and mothers of successful fishermen, who go with their families to fish in the wilds, must know how to deal with the catch. We are not born with this knowledge, somehow we must acquire it. At Camasunary one meets only a few hikers but it is extraordinary how ignorant some of them are.

I was fishing the river there one day when two young men appeared and asked if there was anywhere that they could get a drink of water. I enquired where they had come from. They said Sligachan which was a 10-mile walk along an uninhabited valley. The path passes close by four lochs and crosses innumerable burns. This I pointed out and added that it was all the purest water they were likely to meet anywhere in the British Isles, even if it didn't come out of a tap. When I asked where they came from, they mentioned a town in the industrial midlands. 'Well, when you drink the tap water at home, it has probably been through six people before it gets to you,' I told them. I had recently been talking to a Tweed Purification chemist and thought I should pass on the information he had given me.

A few days later a couple of foreign extraction knocked on the door of Camasunary house, and the man asked politely, 'Whether the lady might use the toilet?' This left even me speechless, and I pointed silently to the appropriate door, marvelling at the fortitude with which she must have shunned the innumerable boulders on her long walk.

One day I was carrying a landing net full of finnocks when I met a young couple who were camping. We passed the time of day, and they seemed nice, so I offered them some fish for supper. The girl looked at them a bit dubiously and asked, 'Are they filleted?'

We all have to learn. There are quick and easy ways of dealing with fish which are well worth knowing. One thing is certain; if you are on a fishing holiday you want to spend the maximum time fishing and the minimum preparing and cooking meals. The object must surely be to produce the best possible food in the shortest time, however primitive the cooking arrangements may be. Fortunately Calor gas has now penetrated almost everywhere. It is so clean and easy to cook with. The roar of the Primus stove, the smell of paraffin throughout the house and the black soot on all the pots and pans are now but memories.

To prepare fish the first thing you need is a small kitchen knife with a sharp blade and point. Split the fish from the vent—the only opening in its stomach—to the head. Then, starting at the back of the head, cut it off and remove the guts. This can be done in one motion if you cut the body side of the piece of cartilage which is attached to the front of the body, and lies beneath the gill cover. You also cut the body side of the two little fins on the body just behind and below the head. The only time when you must leave these all intact, and cut the head side of them, is when you are preparing a salmon for smoking. During this process the cartilage is essential for suspending the salmon in the smoke.

Beneath the backbone, in the body cavity, is a black line. This is blood. Split the covering from vent to head, scrape it out and wash beneath a tap.

It is my job to prepare all the fish we eat, and cook the

breakfast. Once I know my way round a kitchen I can get up, shave, dress and have breakfast on the table in half an hour, if the fish have been prepared the night before. After gutting and washing fish up to ½lb. I roll them in pinhead oatmeal, put them on a plate and keep them in the fridge until next morning. Fish from ¾lb. to 2lb. I split in two by cutting down along the backbone from head to tail. I leave the backbone attached to one half. There is little point in trying to remove it for it comes out much more easily when it is cooked.

If the resultant halves are too large for breakfast portions, I cut them in two at the dorsal fin, or if these would still be too big I divide the halves into three pieces. You then have convenient-sized pieces for rolling in oatmeal for breakfast or cooking in any other way for dinner.

There is a way of removing the backbone from a ½lb. brown or sea-trout; but first you must leave the gutted fish at room temperature over-night. Next morning you will find that the ribs have begun separating from the underlying flesh. With a thumb and forefinger you can continue this process and work your way down the back-bone separating it from the flesh. You only need a knife to split the skin from vent to tail, and cut off the tail.

A fish so treated is the quickest of all to cook and takes only 6 minutes. I roll them in oatmeal and fry them in well-heated good margarine or butter. After about 3 minutes on each side the oatmeal will be brown and crisp and the fish cooked.

Whole trout, or breakfast portions, can either be fried in this way, which takes 10 to 12 minutes, or be cooked in the oven which takes slightly longer, perhaps 15 minutes. In either case I like to cook them in margarine or bacon fat. If they are in the oven you can get on with making the toast and cooking the bacon which is so delicious with trout for breakfast.

You can tell in a second whether a whole trout is cooked

right through or not. Look inside it where the backbone disappears towards the tail. This is the last place to be cooked and the blood remains pink until it is done. As soon as it looses the pinkish colour of blood the fish is cooked right through. When cooking portions of a larger fish the time required depends directly on the thickness of the piece. Half of a 1lb. fish takes about the same time as a whole ½lb. fish.

It is most important that a small fish or a piece of fish is just cooked but not overcooked. When we were children a faithful stalker's wife used to cook the breakfast at Camasunary. Her porridge was fabulous, but one woke to the sound of fish frying and it continued for over half an hour until the result was completely dry and tasteless.

If you want to cook individual portions of fish of over 4lb. you can cut steaks. I take them from near the dorsal fin and cut them about 1½in. thick, or thicker depending on the size of the fish and the anticipated appetites. They take 8 to 12 minutes to cook in a frying pan, under the grill, or in a smoke box.

I can now manage to cook all meals on my own if I have to; but I could hardly make a white sauce before we were married. I don't much like cooking, and after breakfast I am only too delighted to hand over command in the kitchen to Brenda. If there is nobody else around I don't mind hovering about and doing the menial duties of a kitchen maid. Bren understands and enjoys consulting those massive, solid tomes one finds in kitchen drawers, and the slimmer more elegant cook books which are now appearing. She is interested in cooking and is also a fearless improviser.

One day, when we were having lunch in a smart restaurant in Edinburgh, I was rather hurt when I noticed that she was paying no attention to what I was saying. Then I saw the reason. At the next table a waiter was ostentatiously making a sauce to pour over a lobster cocktail. Bren was memorising every detail, the clever girl. We usually manage to catch enough lobsters in Skye to bring back half a dozen at the end of our holiday. When we got home from Edinburgh we took a carton from the deep freeze, and Brenda made the sauce she had memorised. It was quite delicious and cost only a fraction of the price in the restaurant.

Many a time I have asked, 'What's for supper?' knowing that there was nothing in the fridge, but she is never beat, and always produces something good in the miminum time and with no fuss.

When I open a recipe book one of the things that intimidates me is the great number of ingredients of which I have never even heard. Brenda can find her way through this maze with calm ease, and omit all but the essentials which are vital if you want to cook fish in varied and interesting ways. She enjoys producing novel and delicious dishes in a short time when out in the wilds. Over the years she has become adept at this, and the suggestions which follow are the results of her experience.

At Camasunary we have to limit the amount we take as everything, including sheets and clothing, may have to travel 3 miles in a sack across a pony's back. A list of what Brenda takes for making her fish dishes may be of interest. It may appear rather formidable but everything can be packed into quite a small space. She always takes flour, oatmeal, Marvel dried milk, salt, pepper, mustard, anchovy essence, curry powder, rice, olive, corn or other vegetable oil, tins of aspic jelly granules, tinned grilling mushrooms, concentrated mushroom soup; vinegar, a good mayonnaise, Worcester sauce, white wine, P.L.J. (lemon juice), margarine, bacon, cooking cheese, eggs, tomatoes, apples. All these can be incorporated in fish dishes or used for other culinary purposes.

Most of the dishes she produces are made with fish which has been cooked previously. You can either boil large pieces of fish or cook them in tin-foil. Whichever you do, always wash the piece first in cold water with a handful of salt and some vinegar added. This removes all the slime or mucus, and the fishy smell. It then keeps much better if it is sent away by post, and it doesn't smell so nasty when it is boiling.

When boiling fish put some salt in the water and allow the fish to simmer only—for 10 minutes to the pound plus 10 minutes. Then let it cool in the water in which it was cooked.

We now prefer fish which is cooked in the oven in tin-foil. Wrap it up carefully so that it is completely enclosed, and put it in a fairly hot oven for 15 minutes to the pound plus 15 minutes. Fish cooked in this way retains all its flavour and is much firmer than boiled fish.

Kedgeree

We are not very fond of hot boiled salmon or sea-trout, and only the very best should be served cold. There are so many ways of making up fish. I shall mention only a few, but one of the most delicious is the old nursery dish of kedgeree.

Boil some rice, a handful per person, for 20 minutes. Pour into a sieve and run cold water through it. Then make a white sauce, mix in the rice and season with pepper and salt, and put in a double saucepan. Finally add the cooked, flaked salmon or sea-trout and mix gently. Never stir violently or it ends up looking like a pink pudding. Serve with chopped hard-boiled egg and crisp bacon.

If there is any left over it is easily re-heated in the double saucepan; but it is surprising how much people eat if it is made in this way.

One winter when Bill was a little boy and had been unwell, he said he thought he would like some kedgeree for his first proper meal. Brenda went and bought some expensive fish from a shop in Jedburgh and produced it

G*

for lunch. Bill took one look at it and said, 'But that isn't kedgeree: kedgeree is pink.'

Fish for Supper

There are many supper dishes made with a basis of cooked fish flaked into an open fire-proof dish. You can add chopped hard-boiled eggs, with or without tomatoes and fried mushrooms. White sauce made in the usual way with butter or margarine, flour and milk, is poured over, and cheese is grated on top. The dish is then put in the oven until it is hot, and finally the cheese is browned under the grill. You can vary the sauce by adding anchovy essence, or a little curry powder, or mayonnaise with a dash of Worcester sauce added to it. If you are having mushrooms fresh ones are best, but if you can't find any, the small grilling kind are very good. The liquid makes a good addition to the sauce. If you are really pressed for time because fish can be seen rising, a tin of condensed mushroom soup makes a good sauce all on its own.

Fish in White Wine

On a wild wet evening, when there is more time for the cuisine, there is a way of cooking fish in white wine. Sea-trout or brown trout can be used for this. Put uncooked pieces of fish in a casserole and almost cover with white wine; sprinkle with salt and pepper and add a little butter. Cover tightly and put in moderate oven until nearly cooked. Then remove the skin and bones from the fish. Make a white sauce, using the liquid the fish was cooked in with a little milk, and mushrooms if possible. Pour it over the fish, return it to the oven and heat without boiling.

Fish in Aspic

On a fishing holiday two hot meals a day are 'all the

human frame requires', but one is apt to get a bit peckish between breakfast and supper, and a cold dish is then most useful. Cold salmon or sea-trout with mayonnaise is always a standby, but fish in aspic looks very nice and tastes delicious. Make it in a basin using large flakes of fish, add chopped hard-boiled eggs, tomatoes and cooked peas if there are any around. Cover it with aspic, and turn it out next morning when it has set firmly. Green salad goes well with it.

Fish in the Danish Manner

Another good way to eat cold fish is the Danish fish dish. It is an amusing challenge for the fisherman too, because you need as many different fresh water and sea fish as possible. Cook them, and when they are cold, mix them together with chopped apples, 'Granny Smith's' preferably, and a good mayonnaise. Pile this up and serve very cold. Home-made soda bread, made with wholemeal flour, and spread with butter goes very well with this dish. It can be eaten as an entrée or the main course.

Potted Salmon and Sea-trout

It can be very useful to have some potted salmon or sea-trout for use if you are in a hurry at any time. A good way to make this is 'Au Citron'. Pound the cooked fish in a mixer, which makes the operation so simple. Add salt, pepper and quite a lot of lemon juice or P.L.J.; then enough butter to make the consistency firm or creamy as you wish. Work the paste for about 15 minutes until it is quite smooth, and add a little cream if you like. To keep it, put it in pots and seal with melted butter. It can then be put in a refrigerator or deep freeze where it will keep for some time, but not too long, without deteriorating.

It is good as an entrée with hot buttered toast, and excellent on picnics.

How to Smoke Fish

It must have been a great day when primitive man discovered how well the aroma of wood smoke mingled with the flavour of fish. I am sure that primitive dogs clustered around just as mine do when I am cutting up smoked salmon. There are bits I must discard, and the dogs are terribly greedy about it; but it is a mistake to give them too much as they get wildly thirsty with the salt and 'want out' all night.

There are two different ways of smoking fish. One method is to cook fish in hot smoke. With the other they remain uncooked and are cured in cold smoke after being salted.

Cooking fish in smoke is a comparatively new method for most of us. It has been made popular in Britain by the sale of smoke boxes here made by ABU of Sweden. You can get them in most tackle shops. The box comes complete with instructions, a bag of sawdust, and a tin for holding methylated spirits to heat the box. It produces the most delicious fish; but there are two disadvantages both of which are very easily overcome. The first is the cost of replacing the sawdust. You soon use up the bagful you got with the box, and the special Swedish sawdust is absurdly expensive. This annoys me as it must really be worth practically nothing. I have experimented and find that any hardwood sawdust, oak, beech or ash is equally good. I suspect the Swedish stuff is ash. I get mine in a sack from the local sawmill and put it through a small kitchen sieve to remove the larger pieces of timber. I occasionally give the foreman at the mill a small red autumn fish and he appears delighted.

Burning methylated spirits is all right if you are out in the open but has disadvantages if you are in a kitchen. It

smells pretty nasty and covers the outside of the box in
soot—a great nuisance when it comes to washing up. The
container holds enough meths to burn for about 9 minutes.
This is the right time for cooking a ½lb. trout. To cook
a fish of ¾lb. you have to refill it.

Any other form of heat for cooking is preferable, so long
as you know the time required to cook different sized
pieces of fish. There is no problem if you use domestic or
calor gas; but with an Aga or electric stove the box takes
longer to heat up and you must take the time from when
smoke begins pouring from the box.

A whole fish weighing up to ½lb. takes 10 minutes to
cook. A ¾lb. fish takes 14 minutes; but allow a little longer
if you have stuffed as many fish into the box as it will
hold.

The fish should be dried and sprinkled with salt just
before you cook them. Never put salt on earlier as it draws
moisture from the fish. For drying, kitchen paper, usually
known as elephant bumph, is excellent, and can be found
in most kitchens nowadays.

When smoking bits of fish which only have skin on one
side, it is advisable to have the skin-side uppermost in the
smoker. If the flesh-side is on top it becomes very darkened
with the smoke. When I cook salmon steaks in a smoke
box, which are delicious, I cover the exposed flat tops with
a piece of tin foil.

We prefer to eat fish cooked in smoke hot with melted
butter; but many people like them cold with horse-radish
sauce. One never seems to get tired of fish cooked in this
way, and I look forward annually to sea-trout finnocks,
all steaming and golden brown from the smoker. The
whole process is so quick and simple that practically every
fisherman now has an Abu smoker.

Not nearly as many people smoke their own salmon. It is
not such a simple process, but equally worth doing if you
catch enough large fish. Smoked salmon is very expensive
to buy; but the saving in smoking your own is not as great

as one might imagine. From a 2olb. fish you only get slightly under 1olb. of smoked salmon. So smoked salmon must cost more than twice as much as fresh fish if you add on the cost of smoking and transport.

The real advantage of smoking your own is that you can get them exactly as you like. You may not legally sell the large autumn fish you catch on the Tweed, fresh or smoked; but when smoked they keep much longer, and make very acceptable presents. If you send many away to be smoked it becomes expensive, so I enquired of people who did their own, and experimented until finally I have learnt how to do it to my own satisfaction.

The whole process takes time, about half an hour per fish, spread over two or three days, but it is really very simple and requires no expensive equipment. The finished product varies according to the fish you start with. A fat 2olb. springer is the best; a lean 1olb. autumn fish will not be nearly as good when smoked, but even then they do vary quite a bit in a way that is unpredictable. You really have to sample a bit before you know just how good it is. When I have finished smoking five or six fish I take little samples from each and we compare them, the dogs in hopeful attendance.

The process is the same for all fish. Remove the head, gills and guts, leaving the cartilage flap and fins on the front of the body intact. Next remove the backbone with a long and very sharp knife. First cut down on to and along it starting at the head; but don't press down too hard or you may cut through it. Then wearing a rubber glove on the left hand, hold the backbone down and cut up and along it. It takes practice to do this neatly and leave the minimum amount of flesh on the bone.

I then rub coarse salt into the skin, and put the two boneless sides in an old hip bath, skin side down, sprinkle the flesh with a good covering of the salt, and leave it for one hour per pound of the original weight of the fish.

When salting more than one fish, each of different weight, it is important that they are put into the salt at different times, for they must all come out at the same time and go into the smoke without delay. This sometimes takes quite a bit of calculating if the fish vary in weight from 8 to 25lb. If you leave the fish lying around after salting they go a dreadful putty colour. I once delayed the operation over a weekend and ruined three fish.

Liquid is taken from the flesh by the salt as the salt penetrates, and the flesh becomes slightly firmer. The speed at which this happens varies with the temperature. In very cold weather you may have to leave the fish in salt for longer than 1 hour per pound. With practice you can judge the saltiness by the amount of liquid which has been withdrawn, and the texture and feel of the flesh. By altering the time the fish is left in the salt you can get the smoked salmon more or less salty to suit individual tastes.

When salting is complete, make a hole just behind the piece of cartilage on the front of the body, and put a loop of baler twine through it, so you can suspend it from a nail. Then wash all the salt off under a tap, and let it drip-dry for a few minutes.

Any small outhouse with a concrete floor makes an adequate smoke house. Mine is a small brick coal shed. It has wooden beams holding up the roof into which I drive the nails for suspending the fish. The only trouble is that the dailies refuse to go in to collect coal when smoking is in progress.

Any hardwood sawdust makes admirable smoke; it burns better if it has been stored in a dry place for a month or two after cutting. I make a sausage of sawdust about 1ft. deep and 4ft. long, and light one end, using little bits of peat and a Calor gas poker. But twigs and paper are equally good. When the fire is going, blow out the flames, so that it just smokes, and suspend the salmon with their tails about 3ft. above the sawdust.

One other piece of equipment is essential if you are to sleep that night. You must have something to stop the fish from falling in the fire if the string or flesh breaks. The joiner made me a frame with four legs, covered with wire netting about 2ft. from the ground. Brenda made me get this after I had a disaster with a salmon which I was smoking for a friend who had kindly given me a day's fishing.

The sawdust usually smoulders for about 48 hours, which is the time I like to smoke fish for. It if burns too quickly, or you want the salmon smokier, you can renew the sausage of sawdust, and make the fire burn back to where it came from.

Sometimes in cold weather the skin does not dry in this time. You can ensure that it does by laying it skinside down on the wire netting in a gentle heat from the fire. But don't put it too close or it will cook.

When it has finished smoking it looks much nicer if you trim it up, removing all bones and fins. This is the time to taste it, and decide which ones to give away and which to keep. Finally put some olive oil on it to stop it drying, and wrap it up in grease-proof paper.

Smoked salmon will keep for about 3 weeks in a cold larder, but it is apt to go mouldy. It keeps for 6 weeks in a refrigerator, and I keep mine for about 4 months in a deep-freeze. But the best smoked salmon of all is a good fish the moment it comes out of the smoke house.

You can smoke fish of any size, but it is hardly worth doing one of less than 8lb. because each smoked side will only weigh 2lb. I have never done sea-trout in this way, but am told they are very good.

Another recipe

I have one final old West Highland recipe, which I admit I have never tried, but you may like to one day. It emerged during a confidential conversation a friend of mine had with a crofting gillie. The conversation went something like this:

Donald remarked, 'Do the likes of you ever eat potato soup?'

'Oh yes, Donald, often. It is very good.'

'Well it is much better if you put a cormorant in it. Only first you must pluck the cormorant, and to pluck a cormorant you need a pair of pliers. The feathers come out easier if you put it in water with a handful of soda.'

It was not made quite clear if it was washing or baking soda, or whether it went into the soup as well as the cormorant. You would have to experiment. If you ever do I should be interested to know your conclusions.

THE LOBSTER AND THE POT

YOU CAN TELL that we are a seafaring race if you look at the stream of cars going north over the border into Scotland during the summer, and count the ones that have boats, bottom side up, fixed on to their roofs. It is only a pity that the whole contraption can't be turned upside down to avoid frustrating delays at ferries.

Although rowing or sailing on the sea is great fun, there is not much else to do, when you have got somewhere, than to turn round and come back again. It is much more fun if there is a definite object in view. I know that if I was in one of those amphibious combinations, I would spend some of the time afloat trying to catch my own lobsters.

Lobster is one course on the menu in a restaurant or hotel which few of us can afford except as a great luxury. If you want to buy one from a fishmonger it costs more per pound than salmon, and you have to pay for its inedible shell as well. But unlike salmon, which are strictly preserved, you can fish for lobsters anywhere you like round the entire coasts of Britain. Nobody can interfere or stop you. There is a particular satisfaction in pulling up several large lobsters in your own pots if you are as greedy about them as I am.

To catch a salmon you need wealth and skill. To catch lobsters you need neither, and only very little knowledge. I can't think why more people don't have their own pots. All you need is a pot which a lobster can climb into with ease, and out with difficulty. There are firms which make folding ones which you could stow inside the boat on the car's roof. Or if you go to the same place in the Highlands each year for a sea-side holiday, you may easily find a friendly local who will hire or make you some pots. If you have more than one pot you can either tie them together on one string, about 24ft. apart, with a buoy on 60ft. of rope at each end, or have a buoy for each pot.

Unlike when you fish for salmon, bait is no problem. Lobsters will eagerly seek out any flesh or fish, fresh, salted or in a tin, which you lower down into the sea for them. We used to use rabbit when they were plentiful. Some people prefer salted fish as it appears to attract lobsters, but not so many crabs. The cat food Kit-E-Kat is an excellent bait, as are kippers, if you can't catch fresh fish. When using tins, puncture a small hole or two in both the flat sides of the tin, so that the aroma, which so clearly attracts cats and lobsters, can escape a little at a time. But try not to get it on your fingers or clothing, for it has not the same appeal for us humans. But I did hear of a Chinese restaurant which served it to the guests. One tin will last for a long time, for no lobster, however powerful and determined, can open the tin further to devour the bait.

Catching fresh bait is less expensive, and can be part of the fun. There are innumerable fish of many different kinds in the sea. Nearly all can be caught on a bait if one has the knowledge. Some can be caught with comparative ease either on rods or handlines. For catching lobster bait all you require are strong handlines, some leads, 30lb. breaking strain nylon, and a selection of artificial sandeels and spinners.

You may catch fish at any time of day, but they take best when the tide is low and beginning to make in the evening or on a dull day. You catch lythe or saith in 12 to 40ft. of water over seaweed. You catch mackerel, if you come across a shoal, either inshore or further out fishing with six or more flies and a heavy weight lowered vertically from a motionless boat.

Saith are usually 1 to 3lb. in weight and are often caught in great numbers with stiff rods and large flies. But you sometimes hook an enormous lythe on a sandeel. If you do you simply must hold him hard even at the risk of being broken, or he will dive into the seaweed and never come out again. A lythe of 8 to 10lb. pulls very hard indeed at first, and is a great thrill even on a handline.

Sometimes you see things that are far too big to attempt to catch. One day I saw the fin of a basking shark coming towards the boat. It was passing about 10 yards away when Michael happened to say, 'You know, it is a funny thing, but I have never seen a basking shark.' I said, 'Oh, really!' and just pointed. It was about as big as the boat.

Last summer when Brenda, Bill and I were out we saw three pairs of what we later identified as Risso Grampus. They were mothers and quite small children, and they swam close round the boat for about 10 minutes. They were clearly visible for most of the time when they were submerged, and audible as they rose in pairs to blow; their little eyes visible just above the surface. It is always worth while taking a small pair of binoculars on these expeditions.

Lobster pots may sometimes catch their own bait. You often catch dog-fish, which aren't very good as bait; and sometimes you find a conger-eel, wound up like an animated watch spring, in a pot. If the sea is rough and the boat small and full of children, don't release the conger in the bottom of it and attempt to dispatch it with the handle of the oar. To deal with it you need a large sharp knife with a blade that locks open. If you haven't got one put the pot back and hope the eel will find its own way out. If you have, cut off its head before taking it out of the pot. It will still fly around the bottom of the boat, but at least it can't bite. When it calms down you can cut it into segments (for bait).

One day when gazing down I saw what I thought was a motor tyre. Then it moved and I realised that it was an enormous conger-eel.

We were brought up on stories of mermaids and water-horses told by the keeper Peter Macintyre, who was a prince of story-tellers. Small boys covered mile after weary mile without feeling the least tired when listening to him.

He had one grim tale about a conger. Two crofters from Elgol once caught a huge one just before going home. They cut it in half, each took one and they parted to go their separate ways. The man with the tail reached home safely. The other with the head did not. He was found next morning, and appeared to be resting by the roadside, leaning against the wicker peat basket he carried on his back. He had indeed sat down and rested his head against the basket carrying the conger's head. It had gripped him by the neck through a hole, and he was dead.

Whether true or not it was a splendid story for boys, and made a lasting impression.

Lobster fishing is an ideal occupation for the whole family on a fishing holiday when the weather is hot and sunny, the sea flat calm, and nobody can possibly feel the least sea-sick. Lobsters are found in considerable numbers round all the rocky coasts, reefs and islands of the western Highlands. There are innumerable sheltered bays and inlets where the sea remains fairly calm even in rough weather. It is advisable to put the pots in such a sheltered position unless the weather is very settled, or you may not be able to get to them in a small boat if a gale gets up.

Lobsters mostly live in the 'tangles', the broad flat, dark-brown seaweed, 5 to 6ft. long which just emerges at low spring tide, and grows in water to a depth of 40ft. or so. The pots should be covered by at least 6ft. of water at lowest tides. If they are set too shallow they may be broken up by the waves if the weather gets very rough.

At low tide in calm weather the western sea is usually so clear that you can see the rope from the buoy stretching all the way to the pot. As you pull on it you can see the pot emerge from the tangles. If it is a family expedition be sure every small face will be leaning over the same side of the boat, longing to be the first to cry 'a lobster'. Some must be persuaded to lean the other way or you will upset. The first sight of that dark blue sheen is truly exciting for young and old alike. For the young there is the thrill of catching something for which you hope they have not yet acquired the taste. For the elders there is the anticipation of eating something for which they definitely have.

June and July are not good months for catching lobsters, but you can never be sure when they will 'come in'. Last year Bill and I fished twelve pots blank for a week, then one day we got two. The next day we had ten. August and September are very good months. Fishing twelve pots it is easy to average five or six lobsters a day. Quite often there are more than you can eat immediately. In this case we store some in a spare pot without an 'eye' for them to escape through. Their claws have to be immobilised with string or an elastic band, to prevent them from chewing each other up.

Most professional fishermen move their pots frequently, and sometimes I think it is an advantage to find a reef or patch of tangles that is not fished by other people. But then I don't know. Last summer at Camasunary the pots were left in the same not very good place for a month. They caught six dozen lobsters. In October, after a week with no bait except some rusty tins, twelve pots held eight lobsters, and there were only three of us to eat them . . .

We had three small ones that night, immediately they came out of the boiling water, with melted butter. We burnt our fingers and got pretty sticky, but my word they were good.

Lobsters should be boiled alive, either popped into boiling water, or put in cold water and brought to the boil. I think the former is the least cruel. We boil ours for 15 to 20 minutes depending on the size. Put salt in the water or use sea-water. If one is killed inadvertently by being trodden on in the boat, there is no need to throw it away. It is quite wholesome if cooked within 6 hours of meeting its end, but the texture of the flesh is not the same, nor is the taste as good. After boiling they are usually left to get cold. They keep better if this happens quickly and they are put in a refrigerator. The next step is to remove as much lobster as possible from its shell, and it helps greatly to see an expert doing this. Eat all that comes out of the claws and tail. There is also a lot of good eating in the head, but discard the sac right at the front, and don't eat the tough finger-like pieces on either side near the outer shell.

There are many delicious ways of eating lobsters. 'Take one large cold lobster per head,' is quite a good start. With salad and mayonnaise, there is nothing better for lunch.

Mayonnaise
Brenda makes two different mayonnaise dressings, depending on whether she has an electric liquidiser, or must use a whipper. The first with liquidiser: Take 2 tablespoonfuls of vinegar, 1 egg yolk, 1 tablespoonful sugar, and a little salt, pepper, and dry mustard; mix and slowly add $\frac{1}{4}$ pint olive or cooking oil, mixing all the time.

For the second it is easier with two people, one to beat and one to pour the oil. Using a hand whipper beat up 2 egg yolks, add 2 tablespoonfuls boiling water, then, whipping all the time, $\frac{1}{4}$ pint oil which at first must be poured in drop by drop or in a very thin stream. Next add vinegar, sugar and seasoning.

Among the many ways of producing lobster, I am only going to mention a few which are not so well known.

Lobster with Melon
A delicious way of eating it cold is with a melon. Scoop out the centre of 1 small melon, dice and strain off the

juice in a nylon sieve; then put the melon in a dish. Mix
½ pint mayonnaise and 4 tablespoonfuls double cream,
and season. Pour over the melon and fold in ¾lb. diced
lobster. Put in the refrigerator, and serve very cold. This
dish can also be made using prawns or shrimps.

Soda Bread
Soda bread and butter is very good with all these cold
dishes. Brenda got her recipe from an aunt who came from
Ireland.

Take 1lb. plain wholemeal flour, then sieve together
1 teaspoonful each of bicarbonate of soda, and cream of
tartar. Add then, a pinch of salt and a teaspoonful of sugar
to the flour. Mix to a slack dough with milk fairly quickly,
using a palette knife. Place on a floured baking tin, and
bake in a moderate oven for ¾ hour. When you think it is
nearly ready, tap its bottom; if it sounds hollow it is.

Lobster Omelet
When lobsters have been a bit reluctant to go into the
pots, we make one go a long way by having a lobster
omelet. Cut up the cold lobster into fairly small pieces,
mix into a white sauce and heat. Add a wineglassful of
sherry at the last moment. Make two fluffy omelets,
preferably using two frying pans at the same time. Cook
the tops under the grill. Put the lobster sauce as a sandwich
between them, and eat immediately.

Lobster Cutlets
If there are more lobsters than you really need, try cutlets.
Mix fairly large pieces of lobster into a thick white sauce
with sherry, allow to cool on a plate and divide into the
required number of portions. Roll in flour, egg and bread-
crumbs, and fry in deep fat, just as you would an egg

cutlet. If anybody doesn't like lobsters they can indeed have eggs instead.

Lobster Special
Sometimes you catch lots of crabs and few lobsters. For my final lobster dish you can use either, or a mixture. Use 1 cooked crab or lobster. Make a white sauce with ½oz. butter, flour, milk and cream if available. Chop up the fish and place in a saucepan with a wine-glass of sherry, season with salt and pepper. Stir over a low heat for 5 minutes, then add the sauce and some cooked mushrooms. Mix well and pour into a fireproof dish. Sprinkle with cheese, and put in a moderate oven for 10 minutes. Finally brown under the grill. Some people think that this is one of the very best ways of eating lobster.

A boat is not necessary for gathering much of the seafood available round our coasts. At low tide a large variety of delicious things are there to be picked up. Shrimps are to be found on nearly all sandy beaches. Catching them is really much more fun than making sand castles, and certainly more rewarding. I am unlikely to forget the sight of Uncle A on a hot afternoon, charging about the sand at Camasunary at low tide, up to his ample waist in the sea, in damp pursuit. He had a theory that the faster you went the more you caught, and indeed he had quite a bucketful before he became exhausted. Prawns are sometimes to be found under the seaweed. Quite a lot of skill and guile is necessary to catch them.

Then there are the less mobile shellfish such as winkles and mussels, and even oysters, which the more elderly can catch without wetting their feet. There was recently a considerable export of winkles to France from Skye, until some of the bright boys started putting stones in to make up the weight. Strangely enough just exactly the same thing happened in 1726 at Inverness, as I discovered the other day from an old book I was reading. The French don't appreciate the joke any more to-day than they did then.

Winkles spread on hot buttered toast or stirred into a white sauce and eaten with any fish are very good. But they don't travel well. Brenda once filled a gumboot with some lovely fresh ones to take back to her old Nanny, who was partial to them. By the next evening neither the winkles nor the boot were the least fresh.

Mussels in Batter

I think that mussels in batter are about the best shell-fish dish there is. There are masses of mussels of all sizes round our coasts. There are huge ones in Loch Scavaig. Brenda first removes the barnacles by churning them around in a potato peeler. She then puts them in a pan with practically no water, and heats them. As soon as the steam makes them open she puts them in a colander and runs cold water over them. Next she takes them out of their shells and puts them in a sieve to drain. A batter is made from 1 heaped tablespoonful plain flour, salt, egg yolk and 4 tablespoonfuls cold water. The egg white is whipped until stiff and the batter mixture folded in. The mussels are dipped individually into this, and fried, a few at a time, in deep fat. Cooking fat is much more satisfactory for this than oil; it makes them far crisper.

They are served with bread and butter and lemon juice, or P.L.J. which we think identical.

On a calm day you can see a little way down into the sea and recognise green sand, purple seaweed, sea-urchins and fish. But we only see clearly things that come near the surface. We know so little of this fascinating third dimension. The sky above is deadly compared with the sea beneath, and from the sea we must one of these days feed the nations.